PRAISE FOR *BEAUTIFUL INTERFERENCE*

"In *Beautiful Interference*, Tim weaves together powerful stories from the Bible with real-life stories from his own life in order to take us on a journey. You will be inspired, challenged, enlightened, and called to action. You'll need a few hours once you begin to read, because you won't want to put it down."

— **Josh Ross,**
Lead minister,
Sycamore View Church of Christ, Memphis TN;
Author of Re-Entry: How Pain, Roots, and Rhythm
Guide Us from Darkness to Light,
and Bringing Heaven to Earth

"*Beautiful Interference* is a powerful story of hope and love in a family that's been seeking God all along. So when their son comes out to them, Tim and Robin Hall know no other way but to love, continuing to nurture and support their son. Thank you, Tim, for a courageous story of love and inclusion."

— **Sally Gary,**
Director of CenterPeace;
Author of *Loves God, Likes Girls*

Beautiful
INTERFERENCE

*Learning to Love God with all your
Heart, Soul, Mind, and Strength*

BY

TIM HALL

Deep River
B O O K S

Beautiful Interference

Unless otherwise noted, Scripture is taken from the *Holy Bible,* New Living Translation. Copyright © 1996, 2004, 2015 by Tyndale House Foundation. Used by permission of Tyndale House Publishers, Inc., Carol Stream, Illinois 60188. All rights reserved.

Scripture marked MSG is from *The Message*. Copyright © 1993, 1994, 1995, 1996, 2000, 2001, 2002. Used by permission of NavPress Publishing Group.

ISBN – 13: 9781632695062
LOC: 2019934627

Printed in the USA
2019—First Edition
28 27 26 25 24 23 22 21 20 19   10 9 8 7 6 5 4 3 2 1

Live

Beautifully!

Jim

**For Robin, who continues to teach me
how to love like Jesus**

TABLE OF CONTENTS

INTRODUCTION

*T*he Gospel of Mark is my favorite. The sixteen chapters within its pages are chock-full of the urgency and beauty of Jesus' ministry and life. Many scholars believe it was the first of the four Gospels written, with Matthew, Luke, and John using Mark's narrative as a primary source.

It is interesting how these authors seem to focus on specific word usage in their stories about Jesus. Mark uses the word "immediately" time and time again in his account of Jesus' urgent and continued interaction with his creation. The Greek word *euthus* is the word meaning "immediately" or "continuation." *Euthus* is used some forty-one times in Mark's story. Two examples articulated by Mark are when Jesus stopped the storm from capsizing the boat in which the disciples were sailing (Mark 4), and when he walked on the water after feeding five thousand men (it was actually more, because women and children were not counted). He was also constantly on the go in ministry. Jesus was moving all the time.

Of course, his movement was intentional. Action was Jesus' script; he knew what he was doing all the time. There was nothing accidental or hurried in Jesus' life. However, when we look at our own lives, many times we find a hurriedness—a realization that we've packed so much into any given day, we have no margin for what really matters. And what really matters? Jesus and the type of life he has called us to live out, imitating him in every way.

I mean, finding margin for Jesus is a far cry from where we find ourselves in our personal, day-to-day script. We "immediately" leave one thing to go and do another. Hey, who could blame us? There are only twenty-four hours in a day and our calendar is full—so full at times that we forget to actually focus on the purpose for which we live.

A story in Mark 1 reminds me of my own life. Maybe if you're honest, you can nod your head in agreement right beside me, that it reminds you of yourself as well. Right after he calls people to follow him, Jesus goes to Capernaum, located on the northern shore of the Sea of Galilee. He is in the synagogue teaching on a Saturday morning when a man with an evil spirit begins shouting, "Why are you interfering with us, Jesus of Nazareth?"

Now, I don't want to liken us to a man with an evil spirit living inside us, but think about your own hurried life for a moment. You and I are torn between our daily lives, with needs to be taken care of today, and the life we realize God has called us to live in his Son, Jesus the Christ. Both could live in harmony, but many times our *perceived* need is what is on the calendar today, not necessarily a focus on our relationship with Jesus the Christ.

The kids have to be taken to school, and someone needs to make their lunches. There are dirty dishes piled in the kitchen sink . . . and what is that smell? Great. Someone forgot to take out the trash this morning. Clothes are piled high enough in the laundry room that they have their own elevation marker. Groceries need to be purchased, the oil needs to be changed in the car, and it's July. . . . I had made a pledge back in January to read my Bible every day this year. The guilt sets in that I've not been the follower of Jesus I said I would be because I've been too busy, immediately moving from one thing to another on my calendar.

If we're not careful to take the time to tend to our daily spiritual relationship with God, we can become ambivalent, rationalizing that the "Sunday event" takes care of all our spiritual needs.

I once had a discussion with a dad who made sure his high school daughter was a part of multiple soccer teams. The family was gone many times on Sunday morning. When I asked about their absence, he replied, "We pray before the game." While I applaud the gesture, I'm not sure they truly made time to be spiritually fed.

Like this family and the man in the Capernaum synagogue, we could become disconnected and audacious enough to ask the question, "Why are you interfering with my life, Jesus of Nazareth?"

When one reads through the Gospels, one finds the truth—and that truth is that either your busy life is interfering with Jesus molding you, or that Jesus' call is interfering with your current calendar.

The Gospels are full of mottos to live by and collections of Jesus' teaching and philosophies on life. He continually coaches his followers (us) on how to live life to the fullest. Some of those are easy to grasp. I mean, when Jesus says in Matthew 6:9, "Pray like this," we can look at the five verses that follow—the Lord's Prayer—and wrap our minds around the sentences that interconnect us with our communication to God. I should be giving adoration to God; thanking him for my blessings; asking him for his forgiveness for moments I've made poor choices; praising him for rescuing me. It makes sense to us.

Or consider Luke 12:13–21, when Jesus reminds us through the story of the rich fool that life is not measured by what you own but by your close relationship with the Creator. Jesus asks us to reflect in honesty where the longing of our heart is placed—because where our treasure is, Jesus says, we'll find our heart.

But then you have Jesus' words that have been somewhat elusive to me over my Christian journey. When I say "elusive," I don't mean that I do not understand what I'm supposed to do . . . but what *exactly* does Jesus want me to do? As you read through three of the Gospels in the New Testament, you find that the followers of Jesus—a Jew named Matthew, and two Gentiles named Mark and Luke—include this interaction in their storytelling of the life of the Son of God. For our purposes, I want to focus on Mark's rendition of Jesus' teaching because Mark seems to be more inclusive about what Jesus is calling us to live out in our own lives.

Mark includes four areas of life, rather than just three. He records for us Jesus' spoken words in Mark Chapter 12, verses 29–31 (emphasis and bracketed text mine).

> Jesus replied, "The *most* important commandment is this: 'Listen [God's children]! The LORD our God is the one and only LORD. . . . You must love the LORD your God with all your heart, all your soul, all your mind, and all your strength.' The second is *equally important*: 'Love your neighbor as yourself.' *No other commandment* is greater than these [two]."

Okay, okay, you've read that probably a hundred times in your faith journey. But go back and read it again, right now—slowly, unhurriedly, out loud so you can hear your own voice.

Circle the words that stand out to you. (I'm pausing for you to do this.) Now that is rich teaching!

I am a fourth-generation preacher. My great-grandfather "Pappy" Webb became a Christian as an adult in West Tennessee, and began preaching shortly after 1900 at Webb's Chapel Church of Christ. My grandfather Wyatt Hall and my dad, John Hall, were both preachers in the area of Tennessee as well. I guess I could say working with the local church is in my DNA. Certainly, living out Mark 12 is something I really desire to do.

Love God. Love people. I have heard that text all my life. I happen to agree with every word. There is only one God. He's revealed himself in creation, in his pursuit of humankind through all of history, through his physical representation of his Son, Jesus the Christ, and every day in your life with the guidance of the Holy Spirit.

As his creation, we are called to give him our everything. According to Mark's recording of Jesus' spoken words, that should include our *heart*, our *soul*, our *mind*, and our *strength*. According to Jesus' spoken words, it is not an option—we *must* do it. To be a disciple means emulating what our teacher does . . . being like him . . . acting like him . . . living like him.

Still, the question remains for you and me: What does that look like? How would someone, looking at my life, agree that I have given my everything to love my Creator? How would I, at the ripe old age of ninety-four (I have many years before I hit that magic number, by the way), look back at my life and feel the satisfaction that in every facet of my life, I gave it to God? What would the fruit of my desire to put God first in my life look like?

It doesn't stop with just loving on God. It also means I must love other human beings—no matter their skin color, physical

disability, nationality, socioeconomic status, sexual orienta-
tion, number of tattoos, political party affiliation, preference of
music style (although in my opinion, country music is the best),
marital status—I love people exactly as much as I love myself,
no exceptions.

Alright already, I get that; I understand what Jesus has said.
But what does that look like, as it comes to realization in my
own life? How could I feel confident that I am journeying in the
direction that the Rabbi, Jesus, is walking? How could I know
I'm following close behind him? When do I know that his dust
has settled on me?

I believe too many times, as followers of Jesus, we get
wrapped up in the "rule-following" of religion rather than the
tidal wave of love that is Jesus. As followers, we believe that
using the "spiritual clipboard" to check off the things we are
doing or not doing is what God, through his Son, Jesus, wants
us to do. However, based upon Jesus' scathing rebuttal of the
"clipboard checkers" (that is, the religious leaders of his time)
in Matthew 23, I feel God has called us to live a life that many
of us miss—a call to love God and love people with no strings
attached . . . unconditionally. Jesus reminds us to love God with
everything we have, and to love people with that same intensity.

You'll notice that at the end of each chapter I've included
a small-group study, in the hopes that you might explore these
ideas with others in community. Each study should last about
an hour as you dig into the biblical text at hand and discuss
in depth the questions posed after the reading. Along with the
study guide, there are prompts throughout several chapters to
stop and do an exercise. I hope you will take the time to take
some inventory and investigate your spiritual walk, using the
prompts and the appendix in the back.

Throughout this book, and much like Jesus did in his ministry, we are going to use story to help us see the concepts of what God is calling us to do, as we live a life that looks like Jesus Christ. I want us to walk away with a tangible idea—at least a better concept—of what it means to love as God loves us. I want us to feel for God and others as God feels for us. I want us as followers to get lost in the avalanche of God's love for his creation and pursue having that kind of love in our own lives, not only for God but for those around us as well. May the Holy Spirit guide you relentlessly on your way. May you follow the lead of the Rabbi, Jesus the Christ, as if you were his shadow. May God bless you on this journey to which we embark.

LOVE WITH ALL YOUR EMOTION (HEART)

"Create in me a clean heart, O God. Renew a loyal spirit within me."

~Psalm 51:10

"Whatever your heart clings to and confides in, that is really your God."

~Martin Luther, *Large Catechism*

"A loving heart is the beginning of all knowledge."

~Thomas Carlyle, Scottish philosopher

"Guard your heart above all else, for it determines the course of your life."

~Proverbs 4:23

Mark 12:30

"Love the LORD your God with all
your heart (emotion)…"

CHAPTER ONE

TUPOS:

IT'S TIME TO MAKE A MARK

*M*y father started preaching at the ripe old age of sixteen in western Tennessee. His father was a preacher, a night watchman, a farmer, and had other jobs during his lifetime as well. One cold Sunday morning in February 1961, my grandfather was not feeling well, so my dad (who again, was sixteen) was tapped to fill in, bringing the Sunday morning lesson at the small, country church called Burris Chapel where my grandfather preached. That lit the fire for my dad to pursue his calling into preaching. He's been preaching for more than fifty years now.

But there were other influences in his life as well—influences that made him equally desire to do foreign mission work. He prayed ten years for doors to open for him and his family to do overseas work, before anything came to light. Finally, there was an answer to his prayer. He was given the opportunity to do mission work for two years in Kumba, Cameroon, West Africa. So, with my mom and three young sons in tow, my family moved to Cameroon in 1975.

I was a whole seven years old. You remember being seven, don't you? You probably didn't have a lot on your agenda: staying out of trouble, making sure you took a bath like your mom wanted you to do (please use soap), forcing down all the green vegetables you really didn't want to eat. Well, a seven-year-old in Africa . . . can I say it? It was every young boy's dream! It was as if I were the young Indiana Jones (cue the music). Our backyard was a tropical jungle and a cocoa plantation. We owned pets a kid could only dream of in the United States.

I had an African gray parrot that could talk, sounding like the striking keys on my dad's typewriter and the squeaking brakes on his car as he pulled into the carport. Hilarious side story: We had two native African friends down the street named Tee and Taco (you can't make this up). Many times, my friends would knock on our front door to play, stating that we had called them to come up to the house. The reality was, the parrot had learned their names and he began to call them up to the house, with us unaware.

I also had three—count them, three—monkeys: a small, always-agitated monkey named Squeaky, a short-tailed monkey named Hairy (who loved to poop on my middle brother), and a black-haired monkey with a white nose and incredibly long incisors named Akka.

There comes a time in every kid's life when that kid needs to remind everyone with whom they run just how awesome they truly are. Remember? You planned to show the cute neighborhood girl just how strong your muscles were by beating up your younger brother; your best friend just how high you could jump your bike off that ramp you built in the street; or the first time you drove your friends late night to toilet-paper someone's house. The best-laid plans don't always get pulled off how you hoped they would, though. In the end, you could not flex as much as you hoped, you wrecked your bike on re-entry, and you got busted by the neighbors mid-flight of the paper roll you just let sail. Case in point.

After several months of making new local friends, the day came for Timmy-boy (that's me) to prove who was in charge at my house. My parents were not home, so I knew there was no chance of getting in trouble. Famous last words.

All my African friends and I were in the backyard. I climbed up on Akka's wooden crate house on the stump; I sat down on the crate and Akka affectionately sat down beside me. I thought it might be funny to the group if I pushed Akka off his house to have a sort of king-of-the-hill moment. So, like a runner who believes they already have the race won, I smugly pushed Akka off his crate while my friends looked on.

Okay, let's do some fact-checking: Akka is a monkey with basically four webbed hands, who is used to balancing at the tops of trees in the jungle. Did I think a push from me was going to dislodge him from his house? Of course I did. However, Akka barely moved.

With one look from Akka, I realized the gauntlet had been thrown down. Can you believe he had the audacity to look at his "master" with eyes that said, "I really don't think you should do that again"? You've seen that look before—like from your mom or dad when you knew if you didn't stop, there was going to be a whooping of which you'd be on the receiving end.

Of course, for a young American boy in front of his peer group, that meant I had to do it again. So, I pushed Akka again, only much harder, believing that my now eight-year-old muscles would absolutely remove him from my presence and that my stature as king of the hill would be solidified. I'd gather my trophy and be on my way.

As you may have guessed, Akka remained. Only this time, the look he gave me was one of disgust and "I've had enough."

At the age of eight, especially as a male, sometimes (most of the time) you just don't get it. That would be the case with me in this story. Akka warned me but I would not be made a fool in front of my friends. So this third (and later to discover, last) time I stood up. With all the strength I could muster and using my height as leverage, I tried to push Akka off of his house. The Bruce Lee moves of Akka now remind me of Rafiki in *The Lion King* when he and Simba go back to reclaim his throne. With lightning speed, Akka jumped on my left leg and bit a huge chunk of flesh out of my knee. Blood went everywhere—and so did all of my friends! You think you know who has your back, and then discover reality!

You know when you have physical pain, your first automatic decision is to move that pain away from you, so that is what I did. My reflexes told me to push Akka away from my body. In doing so, Akka assumed I was still playing "king of the hill." The push from me prompted another Rafiki move for Akka. He jumped on my left leg again and bit another huge, gaping hole in my shin muscle. By now, my so-called friends were buying popcorn and poking their straws into their forty-four-ounce Slurpee drinks because the show was terrific.

As I pushed Akka away from me a second time, I turned to jump off the roof of the crate on which I'd been a very short-lived king of the hill. As I turned away from Akka, he placed the coup-de-grace by jumping on the back side of my right leg and biting a huge chunk of flesh out of my lower calf, right above my ankle.

I ended up with a tetanus shot and three big butterfly bandages. Why no stitches, you ask? Because you can't sew up what isn't there. The event left an unforgettable mark on my life in two different ways.

It left a physical mark on my body. To this day, I have the scars that Akka gave me. I have the psychological scars as well.

It's very difficult for me to be around animals that have large teeth. So for those of you who know me, it's not that I hate animals, or your dog. I'm just terrified. Thanks to Akka, I have what the apostle Paul calls a *tupos* in my life. The Greek word *tupos* means "mark" or "example."

Paul was making—and receiving—marks for Jesus all over Asia Minor. He represented Jesus in places like Greece and Turkey, Damascus and Jerusalem. Paul encouraged those who heard his story to also make a tupos in life, for the sake of Jesus of Nazareth. Paul sent encouragement in his first letter to the young evangelist Timothy. He said to the young padawan in 1 Timothy 4:12: "Be an example (tupos) to all believers in what you say, in the way you live, in your love, your faith, and your purity." Paul told Timothy, and us, to make an unforgettable Jesus-mark in how we live our lives toward God and how we treat and love one another as God's creation.

Think about your own life for a moment. In the back of this book, write down the top six people who have positively affected your life, and one main reason why they changed you. You cannot use your immediate family members; they are a given. Think about it. Who has made unforgettable positive marks on your life? Don't read another word. Do that right now.

Wow! Now that's revealing, isn't it? You remember those people and what they have done for you because of how they journeyed with you, prayed with you, supported you, cried with you, hurt with you, shared life with you. You will never be the same, because they represented Jesus and have impacted your life.

Those people mean everything to you because they chose, whether they agreed with you totally or not, to stay connected to you. In the words I once heard spoken by the great Bob Goff (author of *Everyone, Always*), "They are tethered to you."

See, when our hearts beat the same, we have deep, abiding relationship. When we have a relationship, we choose to stick together, through thick and thin, whether in storm or fair skies. It's difficult to love someone with all your heart when you don't have relationship—when you're not tethered.

God made that choice to have a relationship with us. Paul says in Romans 5:8 that even while we were sinning, Jesus still died for us. In the storm, in *our* storm, God chose to love by sending himself in the bodily form of Jesus the Christ, and allowed our sin to make a tupos, or mark, on Jesus.

The marks left on Jesus by his death on the cross healed me, took away the guilt of my rebellion, my fault, my stain, and in doing so left God's tupos on me! What joy and happiness I now have because I'm tethered to Jesus Christ. I have relationship with God because of all that Jesus has done for me. What refreshing wind now blows through my soul, as the power of God's love has relationally kept me by his side. How can I not love God with all my heart as my emotions outpour? How can my life not be changed because of the mark Jesus has left on me?

When the depth of what Jesus has done for you registers; when you realize where you might truly be without his unfailing love; when the gravity of God's love pulls you into the peaceful relationship with the master of life, your life changes. When you make a decision to fall in love with the Creator and to love with all of your heart both the Creator and the created, your life no longer uses the script of the world but the red-letter screenplay of Jesus' life. Incredibly, the positive, life-apparent change can dramatically affect those around you—sometimes, surprisingly, those you never even knew were watching.

Early in my ministry career, I worked in Oklahoma as a youth pastor for sixteen years. The last eight of those years, I worked with a church in central Oklahoma that had a great bunch of teens I just loved. These teens were unified, and loved to serve God in various and different ways. They loved to be together. Now, don't get me wrong, they were typical teens. Everything wasn't always a bowl of cherries, but all in all, I loved hanging with them those eight years.

One of the service events we loved to do each summer was an inner-city program called Memphis Workcamp in Memphis, Tennessee. The program generally worked (and still does) in the Orange Mound area of Memphis, a low-income, mostly ethnic part of Memphis. Like all big inner cities, there seems to be a dark cloud of uncertainty with no real felt joy. Drug use is rampant. Violence is ever present. Prostitution is apparent. And in inner-city Memphis, racial tensions are extremely high.

About four hundred teens and adult chaperones come together in one week to paint and repair about twenty-five to thirty houses. That's an incredible amount of work for teens (who pay to do this), who come together, unified to help others who can't help themselves.

The families that live in these neighborhoods are predominantly on fixed incomes and cannot afford to buy the paint needed to put on a fresh coat, fix the steps on the front porch, or replace areas of rotting sideboards. So, trying their best to love God with all their hearts by loving their neighbors as themselves, these kids meet up every summer to do what most of us will not.

Our youth, many times, remind us adults how to live out that change that Jesus creates in us. Paul reminded us what change looks like in our lives when we choose to be in relationship with Jesus, when we are actually different because of what Jesus did for us. He says in Romans 12:9–16,

Don't just pretend to love others. Really love them.
. . . Love each other with genuine affection, and
take delight in honoring each other. . . . Work hard
and serve the Lord enthusiastically. Rejoice in our
confident hope. Be patient in trouble, and keep on
praying. . . . Practice hospitality. Bless those that
persecute you. . . . Live in harmony with each other.
Don't be too proud to enjoy the company of ordinary people. And don't think you know it all!

Fast-forward with my youth group to about 2004. Close to
four hundred teens were divided into groups of twelve to fifteen
to do house painting and light carpentry. This particular year,
one of my youth deacons—we'll call him Larry—was the leader
of one of these groups. It was about 11:30 a.m. and the group
had taken their lunch break in the shade at the house where they
were working, when Larry noticed a big Cadillac pull up by the
curb. Two very large men got out and sat on the hood of the car.

Five long minutes rolled by. Larry was still observing the car,
realizing that the safety of his group was in his care. Suddenly,
the two men slid off the hood, walked to the back of the car,
and opened the back passenger door. A large man, about six foot
seven, got out. He was so large, once he was out, the car sprung
upward like bread jumping out of the toaster.

The three men from the Caddy began to walk toward the
youth group, which alarmed Larry, who left his seat to meet
them halfway through the yard. Now, Larry is a friend of mine
and he's not a small guy either, but on meeting the guy from
the back of the car Larry's eyes hit about the Uber passenger's
neckline.

Larry introduced himself. The passenger introduced himself as "Orange."

This is a title given to the guy who controls all of the crime in Orange Mound—simply "Orange." If you carry that title, you're the kingpin. Everyone answers to you.

Well, Larry was pretty nervous, and asked in the nicest Oklahoman way how he could be of service to Mr. Orange. Orange proceeded to calm Larry's fears.

Orange said in no uncertain terms, "I know why you are here. I know you are sharing love with my neighborhoods. I know you are helping my people. As long as you are here, you will not have one ounce of trouble. Thank you for all you are doing to help." And at that, he walked back to the Cadillac and drove away.

Now I would venture to say, these young Jesus-followers may have hoped to touch someone as hard as Orange but they never thought it probable. My point to telling this story is, again, about living in a way that creates a loving relationship with those around you and with God. When you choose to love unconditionally, anything is possible! Do you believe that? Jesus himself reminds us in Matthew 19:26, "With God everything is possible."

Have you ever thought about the idea of "everything"? Did you know everything means, well, *everything*? Think about three components of your life right now that are not exactly where you'd like them to be. Go to the back of this book and write them down. Go ahead, I'll wait.

Okay. Do you believe God is in control—really in control? Have you prayed about those things like you really do believe that? Give those to God in prayer right now . . . don't wait.

Remember, he's told us, if you believe, you can move a mountain (Mark 11:23).

Now that you've prayed for those things, what about the other things? What other things, you ask? Those would be the things that you don't think of, have not yet thought of, or have not even come to be yet.

Consider what effect your following Jesus will have on your great-great-great grandkids. Remember my "Pappy" Webb in 1900? How he must have prayed for his family to come to follow Jesus. Or what if you went into every restaurant with the idea that God actually could use you in that setting—every . . . single . . . time? Or what if you decided to move forward with a passionate ministry idea, although no one seemed to care whether it succeeded or failed?

See, "everything" means everything—even what you couldn't possibly imagine. You are called to make a mark for Jesus in every facet of your life. I know, it totally blows my mind as well.

Love the Lord with all your heart—and equally important, the people you rub elbows with as well. Don't hold back. Be brave. Do not fear anything. Love recklessly. Give away love. Smile every day. Live like Jesus. We are not called to judge or browbeat or check off any list on a clipboard. We are not called to vet people at the front door. We are called to love. Period. God is love. We are called to imitate him. We are called to make a mark—to be a tupos for the glory of the Rabbi from Nazareth.

No matter what people do, love them, and you'll love God by imitating him. Don't you know imitation is the greatest form of flattery? Flatter God like you have never done before! How will you start today living differently than you did yesterday to make a positive change in your story for the glory of God? Don't hold back. It's time to make the mark.

Study Guide for Chapter One: *Tupos*

Read the text:

1 Timothy 4:12b:

Be an example to all believers in what you say, in the way you live, in your love, your faith, and your purity.

Open:

Tell us about a time someone impacted you in a positive way. How did that make you feel?

Dig in:

1. Read Romans 12:1–2. Paul spells out how we are called to live life as disciples of Jesus. How do these verses bring light to that idea?

2. Read Romans 12:9–10. What does it look like to "hate what is wrong" as a follower of Jesus? How do we embrace right living in everyday life?

3. Name ways that we can honor God in the five different ways Paul explains we are called to be an example. How do we do that as spouses? As coworkers? What would that require of you?

4. Read Romans 12:12. As a human being, how do we experience trouble? Is it different as a follower of Jesus?

5. What are good practices or spiritual disciplines to better the way you live?

6. Read Romans 12:13. Hospitality is something of a lost art. If hospitality is something that defines us as disciples,

how can we create a presence of hospitality in our home and life? Why is that important in our culture?

7. Read Romans 12:18. How are love and peace evident if we choose to live how Paul calls us to live?

8. Based upon these five areas of life, if you had three wishes for your church, what would they be and how can you personally contribute to the fulfillment of those wishes?

CHAPTER TWO

DEVOTION:
HOW DO YOU GIVE
UNCONDITIONAL LOVE?

*M*ost of us have someone we would call our best friend. Typically, it's someone with whom we have shared some tremendous life experiences. Maybe you have done tent camping together in some national parks during extreme temperatures. You've told stories under the starlit night together for years. You have cooked over the hot coals of a campfire, shared clothes because someone's clothes got drenched in an unexpected summer storm, and shared the gasoline bill on the highway. You both have stories about the monster fish that got away.

Your best friend knows your waist size and what style of clothes of which you approve. They know your favorite food. They know your Hollywood star crush. They know about the holes in your favorite pair of underwear that you still wear anyway. They know you as well as you know yourself. So right now, in the back of this book, write down your best friend's name, and only one specific and unique reason why you love them.

When you are done with that, text them to let them know how much you appreciate them. I'll wait for you.

I'm certain you have confided in your best friends as well. Your friends know stories about you that would make some folks walk away from your friendship. You've told them of your struggles with tears in your eyes, and they never flinched. In fact, they hugged you before you could even finish telling the story of your pain . . . your grief . . . your struggle. Those are the people in your life who you know love you with all their heart. You have told them about the secret giant that exists in your life. You can count those types of friends on one hand. But that best friend is there, standing by you, loving you, giant and all. How does that make you feel? Safe? Backed? Supported? Important? Embraced? Loved?

There was a giant man who called Israel's God every name in the book except holy. The overgrown man was not an Israelite. This oversized bully of a man lived in Gath, Philistia. His name was Goliath. Now, if you've grown up in church at all, you've heard the story of David and Goliath, found in 1 Samuel 17. If you haven't read it, do so some time soon. It's incredible. But have you heard of David's soon-to-be best friend, introduced in 1 Samuel 14, just before David really comes on the scene?

Philistia was a country of city-states bordering on God's country of Israel. The coastal country was located right on the Mediterranean Sea, to the west of Israel and the soon-to-be capital of Jerusalem in Judea. Philistia was always crossways with Israel. Philistia was always coming in to roust the local population, plundering and stealing from small Israelite villages and God's chosen people, Israel. Israelite leadership was always trying to choose the best ways to defend their people.

The first king of Israel was a guy named Saul, who became king around 1052 BCE. King Saul was constantly at war with Philistia because they shared a national border and the Philistines did not like Israel being a prominent power in the area. Have you ever been outside, just trying to enjoy the game, the campsite, the evening walk, but the bugs keep hitting you in the face and buzzing in your ear? It's annoying, to say the least. That's how Israel felt about Philistia. There was always trouble between the two countries.

But this story is not about King Saul—it's about his son, Jonathan, who ended up being the best friend of David, (spoiler alert) the guy who killed Goliath. David knocked Goliath out with a stone from a slingshot—and while Goliath was down, David cut off his head! I mean, who says the Bible isn't exciting? But before David came on the scene, Jonathan had a best friend. Jonathan, being a prince and all, had a close confidant and friend, who was also his armor bearer when they went into battle. For our story, let's call the armor bearer Douglas.

So, what does Douglas the armor-bearer do? Well, duties would include refreshing and encouraging your officer; keeping watch as he slept; protecting him at all costs, including watching his back in battle; making sure every piece of equipment was clean, dry, and serviceable; and being a sounding board in strategic plan-making, just to name a few.

In 1 Samuel 14, the Israelite army is in camp in Gibeah, located in the land of Benjamin. Jonathan quietly asks his armor-bearer, Douglas, to go with him to where the Philistines have an outpost, located at the top of two steep cliffs that were side by side. It is just the two of them who leave the campsite. No one knows they have gone, not even King Saul.

Jonathan and his at-the-time best friend make it to two cliffs called Bozez and Seneh. Just above them encamp the Philistia outpost, on top of the cliff. Jonathan is seeking affirmation from God, and wise counsel from Douglas. Jonathan is clearly reminding both himself and Douglas that nothing can hinder victory with the Lord God. He can win a battle whether a few are present or an army is encamped. Jonathan says to his best friend, "Let's go up the cliff and take on these few Philistines in the name of the Lord."

Alright, now let's insert you and me into the story. Now is the time any one of us might suggest we wait, maybe even hold off. We should really think about what is going to happen. We might mention that it's happy hour at Sonic. If we went to get a slushee, we could discuss a plan—or how bad this plan really is and how our mom might not be happy with us for leaving camp. Any one of us might be able to succeed in drawing attention away from our friend's determination.

But Douglas says something that lets Jonathan know he is loved with every bit of Douglas' heart: "I'm with you completely, whatever you decide" (1 Sam. 14:7). Another version of the Bible says, "I'm with you heart and soul." Have you ever loved someone that much? So much that you could say, "I'm with you with all my heart and soul"?

These words sound like what Jesus said about how we are called to love God and each other, doesn't it? To have a friend love you so much that they say, "No matter what storm comes, no matter what you are dealing with, no matter how hard it might be on me, I'm not leaving your side. I will stand with you in the thick of it. I've got your back. If you need to rest, I'll stand watch. Whatever you decide, I'm never stepping away from you. I'm journeying with you all the way."

Life sometimes creates a pause when you realize you have a moment in front of you. A terrifying moment. A moment that could go terribly wrong, or beautifully in your favor. Life reveals a place on the map of your journey where you find yourself at the bottom of the cliffs and the one with whom you are journeying asks, "Do you love me with all your heart? Is our relationship strong enough so that no matter what the story is, I can count on you?" You both know the choice you make will expose how deep or shallow the relationship is rooted.

You have had those unnerving small spaces of time when you revealed something no one else knew, and wondered if those you were telling would truly be compassionate and kind. Would these best friends, these partners in life, stand by you and show you that they loved you with all their heart and soul? Or would they slowly fade away from your life like sidewalk-chalk pictures left in the rain?

Head-rubbing, anxious moments in your life may be memories of the time you revealed an abortion. In the youngness of life, you had no one to stand with you and you made a rash decision that you can never have back. A moment of weakness alone in the house with your girlfriend, and now you are sure you have an STD so you ask a friend to go with you to the doctor. Standing with your hat in your hand, in a moment of worldly passion, you admit a betrayal in your marriage vows. There have been seconds that lasted an eternity when you verbally exposed an addiction to pornography or alcohol or prescription drugs. Even within this heart-wrenching, heart-swelling confession, would our best friends stand with us? As you concede how disappointed you are in yourself, would your friends embrace you and say, "I have your back. . . . I'm not leaving"?

I have been so very blessed to be in so many lives over my ministry career. Numerous situations occurred where a brother or sister in Christ has been at the cliff, asking for wise counsel. I have said to them on occasion and they have equally said to me, "I'm with you heart and soul. Whatever you decide, I am with you. I will not leave you."

Such a moment happened in 2010. My wife, Robin, and I have two incredible sons. As I write this, our youngest, Garrett, has just graduated from Oklahoma State University (my and my wife's alma mater). *Go Pokes!*

Our oldest son, Tanner, graduated from Kansas State University in May 2017. We are a tight-knit family and fully in love with each other, I am proud to say. We actually like hanging out together! All four of us are committed to one another through storm or fair weather. We endured moving to different towns together, car accidents together, girlfriend breakups together (their girlfriends, not mine), painting the house together, and vacationing together. The Halls have been blessed to enjoy life and live through some tough situations as well.

No bigger bottom-of-the-cliff point in my family journey has existed than the one that occurred in the spring of 2010. This is the first time I have openly discussed this story in my life and the life of our family. With grace and love, I have their permission.

Tanner has a quiet personality and is very likeable. He is a kind, gracious, and loving person. Growing up, he was always compliant to his parent's wishes. He is a really good-looking guy. He's a guy you might see as an Abercrombie and Fitch model type. I thought he might actually go into modeling. Hey, I know I have a bias.

Tanner was active in church and the band in high school. He enjoyed being in plays in the community and in school, as did his brother. We traveled together everywhere. One of the beauties of being a youth pastor while your own kids are adolescents is you get to serve with them, mold them, do youth group with them. It is so much fun!

The Halls moved to Overland Park, Kansas to do youth work at a church in 2008. We settled into our rental house and hit the ground running with youth trips, programming, and teaching. It was a great youth ministry and we enjoyed our time there.

But about 2009, Robin and I noticed that Tanner seemed to have a downhearted spirit. He was still a compliant son and respectful, but I could tell he was really working through something. We often talked and prayed together. But Tanner was never one to want to be a burden to anyone, especially his mom and dad, so whenever we spoke about life and how things were going, everything was "fine." What I did not realize was that Tanner was carrying a burden and had been doing so for an incredibly long time . . . on his own.

I will never forget the night in 2010 when Tanner came downstairs to talk to Robin and me. He was sixteen and a sophomore in high school. He had been carrying this on his own since he was in the sixth grade. As he sat in our living room, tears began streaming down his face. He had not said a word yet and Robin and I were already crying as well. When you are with someone, heart and soul, that tends to happen.

With tears in his eyes, he finally let us in on the secret. It was a bomb. He felt he was same-sex-attracted. He had been worried these past few years, first, of what Robin and I would think of him. But secondly, he did not want me to lose my job as a minister of the gospel of reconciliation. Are you serious? You're carrying around the weight of the world and you're worried about your dad. Who does that? Someone who loves you with all his or her heart, that's who.

We talked for some time that night about how long he had felt this way, what his thoughts were about the future, and how God fit into his journey. To help him create avenues to vent his emotions and explore his feelings, Robin and I set up and participated in family counseling over the next two years.

That journey began more than eight years ago, as I write this chapter. As his parents, we continue to journey with him. We may not agree with all the choices those closest to us make in life, but it doesn't mean we leave them or stop loving them or withdraw wishes for a life that exalts God. We love that we have an open dialogue with him concerning all of his life. We have repeatedly reminded him that he is not in this choice alone— that we stand at the bottom of cliff and say, "I'm with you with all my heart. I will not leave you. I love you."

Too many times, we love conditionally. Love with strings attached. Action that says, "I will stand with you as long as you do what I want you to do." But is that the type of love God gives to us? I mean, what sin do you hold in your life? What is the thing in your life that God would say, "Well, that's not what I had in mind for you"?

The Christian community has a few hot-topic buttons that Christians are pushing right now. But what about the stuff common in all our lives, where God shakes his head thinking, "I love them even though they are self-centered or prideful or racist or gluttonous or always angry or mean-spirited or lustful or power-hungry"? The list goes on.

Paul mentions a few of those things in Galatians 5 we often never talk about. Christians enjoy discussing the sin to which they know they are not connected. But Paul mentions quarreling. Do you fight? Do you like to pick fights in church leadership meetings because you aren't getting your way? You explain it away as righteous indignation. Maybe there is some church tradition you fight to keep because it's what you want; it makes you comfortable. So you fight with others who might want something different but still biblical. What about at home with your spouse? Are you so targeted on getting what you want in your home it sparks constant friction with your spouse?

Paul pinpoints outbursts of anger. As a Christian person, have you ever just lost it at work? I know I did, back when I worked as a store manager at Walmart in the 1990s. Embarrassing moments I'm ashamed of as a Christ-follower.

Have you ever gotten angry because the worship music for the Sunday morning event was not where you thought it should be located in the church building? This really happened last year. A lady came up and started yelling at me because the worship music was on the front row and not where she thought it should be. And this lady was just visiting our congregation.

At the end of a tough and tiring day, have you ever just went off on your kids, sending them scrambling in every direction?

Now, I am not trying to make anyone feel guilty. I am as guilty of any of these episodes as the next person. But I also know as a believer in Jesus Christ, the Father has thrown my bad decisions as far as the east is from the west (Psalm 103:12). He has a heart for me. He believes in me. He actually loves me.

Who knows you better than you? No one on earth. You beat yourself up every day because of poor decisions you have made along your journey. Yet, the Father is watching for you from the porch. He longs for you to be with him, no matter what decisions you've made. He loves you with all his heart. He is a giving and forgiving Father who longs to embrace you.

John reminds us that God *gave* his Son so that his creation might once again be home (John 3:16–17). It is through Jesus, not anything we have done, that we are part of God's family. Listen to what Paul writes to the church at Colossae, and to us, in Colossians 1:21–22:

> This includes you who were once far away from God.
> You were his enemies, separated from him by your
> evil thoughts and actions. Yet now he has reconciled
> you to himself through the death of Christ in his
> physical body. As a result, he has brought you into
> his own presence, and you are holy and blameless as
> you stand before him without a single fault.

Although we are imperfect, God has called us his children. He will not leave us. He has not forsaken us. He stands with us at the bottom of every cliff, stating that he's with us heart and soul.

So, what kind of follower of Jesus do you want to be? Heading off to Sonic for happy hour and a slushee—or looking at those who would consider you a friend, knowing you'll be standing with them at the bottom of their cliff, reminding them you love them and that you're not leaving them, and like our example, hugging them up with all your heart?

I can go to Sonic any day. I say we climb the cliff ... together.

Study Guide for Chapter Two: Devotion

Read the text:

1 Samuel 14:1–15:

One day Jonathan said to his armor bearer, "Come on, let's go over to where the Philistines have their outpost." But Jonathan did not tell his father what he was doing.

Meanwhile, Saul and his 600 men were camped on the outskirts of Gibeah, around the pomegranate tree at Migron. Among Saul's men was Ahijah the priest, who was wearing the ephod, the priestly vest. Ahijah was the son of Ichabod's brother Ahitub, son of Phinehas, soon of Eli, the priest of the Lord who had served at Shiloh.

No one realized that Jonathan had left the Israelite camp. To reach the Philistine outpost, Jonathan had to go down between two rocky cliffs that were called Bozez and Seneh. The cliff on the north was in front of Micmash, and the one on the south was in front of Geba. "Let's go across to the outpost of those pagans," Jonathan said to his armor bearer. "Perhaps the Lord will help us, for nothing can hinder the Lord. He can win a battle whether he has many warriors or only a few!"

"Do what you think is best," the armor bearer replied. "I'm with you completely, whatever you decide."

"All right then," Jonathan told him. "We will cross over and let them see us. If they say to us, 'Stay where you are or we'll kill you,' then we will stop and not go up to them. But if they say, 'Come on up and fight,' then we will go up. That will be the Lord's sign that he will help us defeat them."

When the Philistines saw them coming, they shouted, "Look! The Hebrews are crawling out of their holes!" Then the men from the outpost shouted to Jonathan, "Come on up here, and we'll teach you a lesson!"

"Come on, climb right behind me," Jonathan said to his armor bearer, "for the Lord will help us defeat them!"

So they climbed up using both hands and feet, and the Philistines fell before Jonathan, and his armor bearer killed those who came behind them. They killed some twenty men in all, and their bodies were scattered over about half an acre.

Suddenly, panic broke out in the Philistine army, both in the camp and in the field including even the outposts and raiding parties. And just then an earthquake struck, and everyone was terrified.

Open:

Who would you say is your best friend? Why would you say that? What evidence is there?

Dig in:

1. Based upon this story, how important is it for you to have community?

2. Is having a metaphoric battle plan for life in Christ important, or does Jesus have everything figured out so why worry? Explain.

3. "Bozez," translated, means "shining." What "cliffs" require work in your life, but are rewarding and meaningful?

4. Who do you call to journey with you up your "Bozez cliff"?

5. "Seneh," translated means "rocky and thorn-strewn." What "cliffs" will be challenging and difficult in your life? Why is it important to have the right people with you as you climb?

6. Our Christian walk is really all about relationship. Jonathan had a deep relationship with God and with his armor bearer. Discuss how you have deepened your relationship with God. What spiritual disciplines do you use in your life to discover who God is to you and how you can walk closer with him?

7. What intentional things do you do to deepen your friendships? What do you have to do to keep your closest friendships intimate, including the ability to be vulnerable?

8. How does this Old Testament story remind us of our mandate by Jesus in Mark 12:30–31?

Chapter Three

FORGIVENESS:
IT'S TIME TO TRULY LET GO

My dad had three boys, and I'm certain we gave him a run for his money. We were always getting into some kind of trouble that required his attention to get us back on the "right" path. No doubt you have some stories as well.

Jesus tells a story about a father who had two sons, as recorded by Luke in Chapter 15 of his Gospel. It appears there was sibling rivalry and rebelliousness between the two boys. The youngest son was fed up with farm life and doing whatever Dad wanted done. He had grown tired of the dawn-to-dusk schedule with which so many who live on a farm are so familiar. The younger brother was ready to hang up his gloves and mucking boots for more glamorous attire. Besides, the younger son had an older brother who was going to work the farm anyway. So the youngest does the unimaginable: While his dad is still active and living, the young son asks his dad for the inheritance that belongs to him. He wants to hit the road and leave family and farm before he gets another day older.

I have always been surprised that the dad gave it to him. I don't know why I am surprised. It's probably because I put myself in the "dad" spot of the story and think, I would just fall over laughing if my son came and demanded his half. I'd first tell him that his half (a whopping $29.38) would not get him far. And second, "Ummm, get back to work." But then I remember that the dad in Jesus' story represents God. God loves us with all his heart, as he expects us to love him with all our hearts. So, the dad gave the young son what he asked for.

By all accounts, as soon as the son had his money, he loaded down his favorite ride and hit the road to a brighter tomorrow. It was a tomorrow that did not include cowbells, early-morning rooster crows, and the end-of-day stall-mucking regimen. The young one was going to stay up late . . . and maybe never go to bed. He was going to hit the big town and paint it red. He was finally going to do things he had only dreamed about over the last several years. The young son never let the door hit him in the backside. He was gone. And his father, with tears, watched him go down the road in a cloud of dust.

You and I have dreamed some of those crazy, stupid dreams before. I know I have had those dreams that turned into nightmares. You see, I was the stubborn firstborn son of a preacher man who was bent on doing things his way—not Dad's way, or God's way.

From the day I was born, I enjoyed the grace of God. I was born in West Monroe, Louisiana and from the moment the doctor said, "It's a boy!" I was in church. If the doors were open, we were there. If it was grounds cleanup day, I had to be there. If we were singing at the retirement home, I was on the front row. You see, I was the oldest of three boys. The oldest have certain unrealistic expectations placed on them by their parents. (If you are a firstborn, can I get an "Amen"?) I was expected to toe the line, obey my parents with not one word back, look nice and be nice, be seen but never heard.

Dad, the preacher, moved to a different church about every two years, which meant, that's right, his family of course did as well. During my growing-up years, we had the blessing of living in Louisiana, Georgia, Arkansas, Tennessee, Michigan, West Africa, and some then-unknown islands in the South Pacific called Vanuatu. Looking back, all of those moves helped form me into the man I am today. I am ever so grateful for the opportunity to live in and experience numerous different cultures. However, during that period of time, I loathed the moves we made every twenty-four months or so.

Every few months, I was thrown into a new school system with other kids I did not know. It was difficult to make friends, to squeeze into their tight cliques. I was picked on because I was small and naïve. I usually didn't wear the same clothes as my peer group. But eventually, I learned how to operate on my own. I learned that you could not really trust anyone because they leave, or you leave, and the ones you do let in just let you down. You feel lonely and rejected, but on the outside you play tough. You struggle because you are unsure of who you are; you have no roots. At least that's what you tell yourself.

By the time I was a sophomore in high school, I was good at playing like a Jesus-follower because that's what was expected in my house, but I had plans. There was a lot of rule-following at our house. One had to be aware of what other people thought of them, since my brothers and I were the preacher's kids, and so the screws were tight. Oh, I said the right things and in a church crowd, I'd make anyone proud. But deep down, I could not wait to get away and really start living. Starting to sound familiar?

I graduated high school in a small town in Arkansas and initially went to an expensive conservative Christian university in Arkansas in the fall of 1986. My parents dropped off their oldest son in the fall of that year, and my dreams started to become a reality. Now, it took this naïve kid the first semester to realize: I really could make some decisions on my own. I didn't need permission to stay out, or go shopping, or go to the lake. This was starting to feel like freedom. I knew what I had needed all these years. No one else, not even God, knew my best life plan. I had gained information about God. I could quote Scripture. I knew where biblical stories were located. But God seemed distant. It seemed he had not been able to help me all those years I felt so alone and tossed about. Why would he start now?

So I embarked on living life. However, starting the Tim Hall life plan, I spun like a top, going to class in the day, working in retail in the afternoon and evenings—and when off during the week and on the weekends, the life-party was on. Hitting the club scene in Little Rock (hey, it was the closest large town to me). Waking up in someone's house that I didn't know. Not paying the utility bill because I had spent my hard-earned money on what I wanted. I was styling and profiling. Now this was what I always thought it would be. I was making the decisions now. No one was going to tell me where to go or who to be seen with or how to spend my money or what may or may not be good for me. All the authority figures—the figures who cared for me—were out of sight, out of mind. Though this last sentence was true, the inverse could not have been more different.

Remembering Jesus' story in Luke 15, can you imagine what that father went through? Whether you are a parent or not, I know you have been there, second-guessing a decision. You hear the voice in your head battling with heart. At the time, it seemed like the thing to do, so you followed through with what your heart told you to do in that sliver of time. That father in Jesus' story must have stayed up for weeks, drinking coffee late at night, watching reruns of *Parks and Recreation* to take his mind off of the moment, praying that his boy would be all right and that nothing bad would happen to him.

I've often thought the dad in Jesus' story, on a weekend, drove over to where he knew his son was "living" to watch from a distance so he could just see him one more time. Was he okay? Was he eating? Did he remember his dad at all? Does he still know in his rebellion I love him more than life itself . . . that I still love him with all my heart?

In those wilderness years of mine, I know now that God never left me. He had a plan for me, but he needed to allow me some rope so I would see I needed him—so I would see that life without God really is not life at all. Paul reminds us in his letter to the Roman church, "When we were utterly helpless, Christ came at just the right time and died for us sinners. . . . God showed his great love for us by sending Christ to die for us while we were still sinners" (Rom. 5:6, 8).

See, the Father will do whatever it takes to get back his creation. He will go to any length to make sure the son knows he's loved and that someone cares for him. He loved you and me so much he gave up what he loved dearly. He sacrificed in pain to get our attention and show us love. He patiently waits for his creation to hit the bottom of the barrel, when our dreams turn into nightmares.

I finally realized, somehow, that the dreams and self-made plan were not everything I thought they would be. Waking up every morning with no community, no love, no heart after all the money is gone—only realizing it is Monday and that you have to do it all over again this week if you even want an hour of feeling like people care for you. The emptiness of impressing people who don't care about you, the feeling of being used when paying the tab, the loneliness of being in a relationship but having zero community or intimacy with that person. You realize after literally having a knife put to your throat and a gun to your chest, this is not the grand dream you thought of back on the farm. You come to grips with this reality: You, wrapped up in yourself, makes an incredibly small package.

Luke's story does tell us that the father waited daily on the porch, looking down the road to see if his son might possibly be coming home this particular day. We do not know how long it had been, but one day, all the dad's prayers concretized. There in the distance was a small, emaciated, ragged figure of a young man turning the bend in the road. He walked slowly, somewhat slumped. He was embarrassed and ashamed. Even with the slowness, the father knew that gait. Could it be? Is it possible that my son could be coming home?

In one great stride, the father leaps from his chair on the porch and clears the extended steps leading into the yard. He had not run this fast in thirty years. As he gets closer to the young man, he slows. This man has a full beard and ratted, unkempt hair; his clothes are full of holes. His face and hands are dirty, as if he had been in the mud with pigs. His feet are bloodied from the blisters of traveling without shoes. They finally are within arm's length, when the young man looks up sheepishly with an expression of helplessness.

The father's heart leaps, and a smile larger than the farm itself appears on his face. The eyes cannot hide who you are. This *is* my son who has come home. But wait, the boy wants to say something. He has all his words prepared. He has rehearsed them for weeks, days, hours, and miles coming home. He has a confession to make. The son wants his father to know he realizes he messed up. He has made deep, gashing relational wounds that will heal but leave scars. He has done unmentionable things with his father's money. He has created disrespect for his father's name. He realizes nothing will ever be the same again. In fact, he knows he will lose the right to carry his father's name and is willing to simply be a servant on the farm. The son confesses all to his father.

But the father will have none of that. My son, my friend, my namesake has come home. Don't you know? I love you with all of my heart! You are everything to me. I've been half of me since you left. I am with you heart and soul. I will not leave you in your weakness. I will not melt away because of your choices. I will stand and fight with you and fight for you. I have your back. I will stand watch while you sleep. You have me on your whole journey, not just when you choose what I would choose.

At the end of Jesus' story in Luke, the son returns home, broken but confessional. He is a different person. He will be an even better person. He has a best friend there who welcomes him home.

I finally came home after five years in my wilderness. I gave up running away. I started running toward the maker of life, Jesus Christ. I rededicated myself to telling the story of Jesus and of the healing power that only he can provide. I had made the poor assumption that I was no longer fit to wear his family name. I had thrown that opportunity away, or so I thought. But he is a gracious and merciful God. I literally cannot believe the blessing I have had now for more than twenty-five years, working in his kingdom. I'm so blessed to be living God's plan for my life, his dream for me.

So what about you? Where do you find yourself in the Lucan story? If you are anything like me, deep down, you know you have been rebellious. You have been lonely and feel rejected. You have been abused. You have felt isolated. Your plan is not working out like you thought it might when you dreamed it all those years ago. You long for community and to feel whole again.

The father is on the porch and he's looking for you. Whatever you believe you have done is not enough to keep you away from him. He's beckoning you: Come home. Don't wait any longer. Embrace the new wonderful story he has for you. Jesus invites you home. Do not do life alone. Do not carry the burden of your poor decisions any longer. He says in Matthew 11:28–29, "Come to me, all of you who are tired and carry heavy burdens, and I will give you rest. . . . You will find rest for your souls."

Isn't it time to come home?

Study Guide for Chapter Three: Forgiveness

Read the text:

Luke 15:11–32:

Jesus told them this story: "A man had two sons. The younger son told his father, 'I want my share of your estate now before you die.' So his father agreed to divide his wealth between his sons.

"A few days later this younger son packed all his belongings and moved to a distant land, and there he wasted all his money in wild living. About the time his money ran out, a great famine swept over the land, and he began to starve. He persuaded a local farmer to hire him, and the man sent him into his fields to feed the pigs. The young man became so hungry that even the pods he was feeding the pigs looked good to him. But no one gave him anything.

"When he finally came to his senses, he said to himself, 'At home even the hired servants have food enough to spare, and here I am dying of hunger! I will go home to my father and say, "Father, I have sinned against both heaven and you, and I am no longer worthy of being called your son. Please take me on as a hired servant."'

"So he returned home to his father. And while he was still a long way off, his father saw him coming. Filled with love and compassion, he ran to his son, embraced him, and kissed him. His son said to him, 'Father, I have sinned against both heaven and you, and I am no longer worthy of being called your son.'

"But his father said to the servants, 'Quick! Bring the finest robe in the house and put it on him. Get a ring for his finger and sandals for his feet. And kill the calf we have been fattening.

We must celebrate with a feast, for this son of mine was dead and has now returned to life. He was lost, but now he is found.' So the party began.

"Meanwhile, the older son was in the fields working. When he returned home, he heard music and dancing in the house, and he asked one of the servants what was going on. 'Your brother is back,' he was told, 'and your father has killed the fattened calf. We are celebrating because of his safe return.'

"The older brother was angry and wouldn't go in. His father came out and begged him, but he replied, 'All these years I've slaved for you and never once refused to do a single thing you told me to. And in all that time you never gave me even one young goat for a feast with my friends. Yet when this son of yours comes back after squandering your money on prostitutes, you celebrate by killing the fattened calf!'

"His father said to him, 'Look, dear son, you have always stayed by me, and everything I have is yours. We had to celebrate this happy day. For your brother was dead and has come back to life! He was lost, but now he is found!'"

Open:

What is the dirtiest or "lowest" job you've ever had? Talk about it.

Dig in:

1. Read Deuteronomy 21:15–21. How does Jesus' story challenge the expectations of the Law? How do you believe the audience would have reacted to Jesus' story?

2. Who is listening to this story (see Luke 15:1–2)? Why is it significant that both ends of the religious spectrum are present?

3. Who do you believe each character represents in the story? Why do you say that?

4. What does the son receive in verse 12? Verse 20? Verse 22? Which do you think he valued more, and why?

5. Compare your situation with the son's journey. Where do you believe you most closely walk in the story?

6. What would you say is the one thing our church can do to most resemble the father in this story? What would we have to change to look like the father?

LOVE WITH ALL YOUR SPIRITUALITY (SOUL)

"O my soul, bless God. From head to toe, I'll bless his holy name!"

~Psalm 103:1 (MSG)

"The soul becomes dyed with the color of its thoughts."

~Marcus Aurelius,
Roman emperor

"The most powerful weapon on earth is the human soul on fire."

~Ferdinand Foch,
Supreme Allied Commander, WWI

Mark 12:30

"Love the LORD your God with all your . . .
soul (spirituality)"

Chapter Four

EXPERIENCE:
HOW DO YOU FEEL GOD'S PRESENCE?

*Y*outh ministry. There's nothing like it. You are balancing your sanity between the interesting smell of junior high boys, the drama of high school girls, and the eyebrow-raised parent who believes their child is *really* the only important kid in the youth group. Many times, I have wondered if I was really doing what God wanted me to do . . . if I had *really* heard his voice above all others when that voice called me into ministry in 1993. In the twenty years that I pastored adolescents (and their parents), I have asked that question openly to God. "God, is this what you want me to do? I feel like I make no difference to the teens and preteens I'm working with. Please confirm in some extraordinary way that I have listened to your Spirit correctly."

Many times after I have prayed, within days I have received a phone call, a text, or an email from a young adult who was in my youth group but now graduated high school, thanking me for the time I spent guiding them and teaching them how much Jesus the Christ loves them. They are now living the adult life. They realize the time that was put into each Bible class, summer camp, seasonal retreat, or activity.

I want you to think about the adult that poured into you during your adolescence. What name just pops into your mind? Which person brings a smile to your face? Whether a paid youth minister or a concerned parent, who do you realize went out of their way to help you through those tough times during your growing years? Who helped you learn who Jesus was, using the most endearing and fun ways? Go to the back of this book and write down that name. Write down how they positively affected you in your walk with God. What actions or words did they speak that made all the difference in your world in those months and years?

Now that you've written that down, take the time *this week* to text, call, or email them. Let them know how much it meant to you that they journeyed with you. You have no idea what an encouragement you will be to them on their journey, just knowing they made a difference in your life. Take it from a guy who has been on the receiving end of those moments. You will make them smile, and probably cry a happy cry.

You know, it is great to get those human affirmations. Have you ever thought about the ways God is giving you two thumbs up? What about affirmation from God—the affirmation that you are making great choices as you do your best to follow him?

Have you ever doubted God? Let's be honest. If you are journeying and feel like you are following the Rabbi from Nazareth, you have had moments when you might have wondered, "Are you real, God? Have you called me to be this person that I am right now? Am I hearing you correctly? Is there something else I am supposed to be doing?"

I think about a small guy from a small family who lived many, many years ago—and who was quite sure God was not talking to him. He was a guy trying to hide from bullies.

Have you ever been bullied? I know I have. If your eyes are open, you will see even in your adult life, bullies exist. I was physically a super-small guy growing up. Living in a different town about every twenty-four months, the bullies on the playgrounds and in the classes of my junior high and high school found it amusing to scare me, threaten me, hit me, take what was mine . . . the list goes on. If you were ever bullied, you know what I'm talking about. One discovers ways to melt into the background, so as not to be seen.

Well I resonate with a guy found in Judges 6 who was bullied along with the rest of Israel for seven years by a group of people called the Midianites. Who were the Midianites, you ask? Well, Genesis 25 tells us that Midian was one of the children of Abraham and Keturah (notice this wife is not Sarai, through whom the child of promise, Isaac, was spoken). The text goes on to say that Abraham, although he gave everything he owned to Isaac, also gave gifts to the sons of his concubines and sent them east, away from Isaac. This group was located in the northwest Arabian Peninsula, east of the Promised Land of Canaan.

The astonishing story of the Bible is so interesting. What you find in the Hebrew Bible—what Christ-followers call the Old Testament—is that the offspring of Abraham are continually cruel, evil, and oppressive to . . . others who are also the offspring of Abraham. It's like the family reunion that doesn't end well. Although the Israelites are the chosen family through which the Messiah (Jesus) is to come, the Israelites keep ignoring what God has told them to do and how to live—so God allows another distant family member to have their way with the chosen family, in order to get their attention.

Okay. Back to the story. The Midianites ruled over the Israelites for seven years. The story in Judges 6 says that the Midianites were so cruel to the Israelites that the Israelites made hiding places for themselves in the mountains, caves, and strongholds. During harvest season (April through September), the Midianites would swoop in, taking the harvested crops and destroying the rest. They would also take Israel's livestock. The story says when they came they were as "thick as locusts" (Judg. 6:5)—too many to count. They stayed until the land was stripped bare.

As usual throughout the stories in the book of Judges, the Israelites cry out to God for appeasement and help. God responds in a positive way, but with a warning: He will help them, but they must not continue to worship other gods. He is the God who brought them out of Egypt and slavery. He will save them again.

Enter God's vessel, the human hero of the story: a guy named Gideon. He's the one whom God will use to save the day. He's strong enough that he could have been a Marvel Avenger. But where do we find him in Judges 6? He is hiding at the bottom of a winepress, so he can conceal the grain he's gathering from the bullies. Remember, the Midianites? The angel of the Lord speaks to Gideon and says, "Mighty hero, the LORD is with you!" (Judg. 6:12).

Now, I know you have had moments of question; moments when you wondered where God was in your predicament; moments you thought you were all alone in an endeavor; moments when you wished you confidently knew there was someone to lean on; moments when you questioned if God even knew what you were dealing with in your life. Our human hero is in that same emotional moment. Gideon asks, "Why is all this happening to us if God is with us?"

God simply replies, "Go with the strength you have. . . . I am sending you!" (Judg. 6:14).

Of course, like you and me when we're giving excuses to Mom why we didn't do a household chore, Gideon has an answer for that mandate: "How can I do what you have asked? My immediate family is the weakest in the whole family of Manasseh and I am the smallest, least authoritative person in my entire family."

Then the Lord said, "I will be with you. You will fight the whole tribe of Midianites and it will be as if you are fighting just one man" (see Judg. 6:15–16).

Gideon is a regular fellow just like you and me; he still has doubt. So he arranges a surefire way to eliminate his needing to go anywhere except back to his recliner and his snacks in the bottom of that winepress. But finally, after his evasive maneuvers move Gideon right back in front of God, Gideon sets up a way to see if God is truly sending him.

Gideon asks, "Am I doing the right thing? Have I heard your voice correctly? Are you really sending me?" In the threshing floor near his home, Gideon is saying to God, "Prove it." Prove you are who you say you are. Show me that you are indeed the God of Israel and you will not leave me (and all of us) totally alone. Prove to me you are the God I have heard so much about my whole life.

So Gideon puts a sheepskin on the floor. He tells God that if the wool is wet in the morning while the ground is dry, he'll know God is going to do as he says. And the story tells us that is what happened. It says that the next morning, Gideon squeezed out a bowlful of water. The wool was so saturated, there would be no mistaking God was present. Now, this was a miracle. In the threshing floor, one area was wet while another area immediately around the wet area was not wet. Some of us might have conceded, "I was wrong and the angel of the Lord was right. God is present and hears our cry for help."

But not Gideon. He asks for yet another confirmation. He says this time, "Make the wool sheepskin dry while the ground all around the threshing floor is wet." And wouldn't you know, the next morning, God confirms again that he is walking with his servant.

If we're honest, most of us do the same exact thing. We see God's work all around us, and still need something more to believe. I believe God confirms every day that he is with you and me. But through our stubbornness, we fail to acknowledge his presence.

In the summer of 2001, I took two guys from my youth group to Camp Blue Haven in New Mexico. I had been asked to teach a Bible class at the camp the week we were there. It was the first time either my compadres or I had been to the camp. The camp was gorgeous. Set in the northeastern mountains of New Mexico, the camp was peaceful, with a babbling creek running through the Blue Haven. It was a place where I could ask God some questions, where I would not be distracted by anything except God's voice in my ear. By all accounts, the three of us—Brian, Travis and myself—had a great time that week.

When the warm summer sun peeked through the darkness of early morning, I arose and got ready for the day. Before breakfast each morning, I took my Bible, the book I was reading at the time (Bruce Wilkinson's *The Prayer of Jabez*), and my open heart to the creek to read, pray, and ponder my usefulness in God's kingdom. I was asking questions to God about my life, ministry, direction. Was I doing what he called me to do? Was I the kind of father I should be? Did I really treat my wife as if she were my best friend? Was I effective at all as a minister in a church? Did I fully acknowledge God in my work as a youth pastor? I prayed and asked God questions on Sunday and Monday as I began my week at Blue Haven.

I remember on Tuesday morning, I felt different. I felt that maybe I had settled into church work. I felt maybe I was making it all work out when in fact, God didn't want me in this position. I felt like God was far away, but I wanted to know in no uncertain terms that I had listened to God and sought to be Jesus' disciple by leading adolescents in the way of the kingdom of God.

Again, I had been asked this particular week to teach a Bible class. I was teaching how to listen to God's voice—how to follow him in a world of chaos and noise. My first meeting time with campers would begin after breakfast each day. I had prepared my material but kept my internal questions to myself . . . except for this morning. I laid my questions out to God. And, like Gideon, I wanted some proof that God was actually listening to my prayers, that he had not left me to walk alone. I needed confirmation that he had selected me to be a part of his kingdom in this way.

As I was reading *The Prayer of Jabez*, Bruce Wilkinson reminded me that Jabez's territory was expanded because he'd prayed for that to happen. The text simply and quickly says that God granted Jabez's request.

So, I asked God on that day (Tuesday) to send me an assignment—today. It had to be today, for me to believe that God was indeed listening to me in my prayer. I prayed for God to expand my territory, to send me specific ministry, *today*.

I wrapped up my personal devotional time at the creek and headed to breakfast. I sat with the guys who had come to camp with me and asked how their week was going. Mealtimes were in this grand log cabin somewhat centered in the middle of camp, and everyone saw everyone. After we were done eating and talking, it was off to the first Bible class time of the day.

The teens at camp came slowly walking into this open-air classroom in the middle of the woods. The open space resembled one of the woodland scenes from *The Lord of the Rings*. The campers sat on large stones and wooden benches, while I stood at the apex of the area. The trees around us seemed to hold hands and encircle us all as if joining in as we proclaimed God's majesty in our time together.

By the time I was done with my opening prayer and asking the campers where to turn in their Bibles for today's passage, I had already forgotten about my request to God that morning. I was focused on the task at hand: presenting a lesson on listening to God in a way that would grab these sleepy campers and shake them theologically like ragdolls into the consciousness of God's Spirit. The teaching went on for about forty-five minutes, after which we all left the outdoor, rock-laden classroom for our next event.

But on this day, something went differently. As we left the area, a young seventeen-year-old girl came up to walk beside me. Let's call her Pam. She was a senior in high school. Pam had tears in her eyes. I could tell she wanted to ask me a question, so I opened myself up to listen to her plight.

Pam was upset, and confessed that she did not get along with her youth minister. She wanted to know what she could do to smooth things over. Pam didn't want to be a doormat, but she knew that she had not been the nicest person to him either. They clashed on multiple occasions about different things, ranging from what activities were going on in her youth group to the type of classes he was teaching to the clothes Pam wore. She was very open about all the things they had banged heads over.

So, I gave her some sage advice and a prayer. Pam seemed to be open to trying the things I mentioned, to be the better person Jesus wanted her to be as she interacted—not only with her youth pastor, but with all the people she interrelated with on her journey in life. She moved forward to walk with her friends.

I felt good about the class. It had appeared that my slant on Scripture had aroused in her a desire to look more like Jesus. I felt somewhat satisfied, and with a smile, gave the moment not another thought.

The next morning (Wednesday), I rose with the warm summer sun again to attend to my devotional time by the creek, reading God's Word and praying. I was convinced still that God needed to let me know, without a shadow of doubt, he was listening to my prayer life and hearing my desire to be a part of what he was doing in the world. So, like Gideon, on the second day of my challenge, I asked God again to send a definite assignment—something tangible, a specific moment just for me. (I had still not realized that my Tuesday interaction with Pam was God's first specific assignment, to let me know he was listening.)

After my early morning devotional time by the creek, I went to breakfast to hang with my great friends from my youth group before we ventured out into the day. We had the typical camp cuisine that morning: a bowl of Frosted Flakes, a stack of pancakes, and two chocolate milks. And wouldn't you know it, while I was eating that delicious camp food, a young man with red hair (Philip) sat down across from me at the table . . . only he had no food. Philip was simply looking intently at me when he asked me a question, "Tim, could you meet me on the mess hall deck about 2:00 today?" I assured him that would not be a problem at all, and looked forward to our conversation.

I went to teach my Bible class that morning in my open-air classroom. The day's activities, up until lunch, seemed to drag. You see, I knew I had this 2:00 meeting that the Holy Spirit had set up.

Finally, 2:00 rolled around. I found myself pacing on the deck of the mess hall waiting for Philip, when finally my appointment arrived. I felt empowered as a rabbi might feel when his pupil wanted some solid advice about life.

Philip's question had to do with how he would interact with a friend who happens to be an atheist. He didn't want to drive his friend away, but realized God had put the two of them together in order for him to witness to his friend. I gave him the best advice I could and prayed with him. He went on his way, grateful for my time.

Now every night at Blue Haven, as I would assume it is at most summer camps, we have large group worship time. There is an inspiring message based around the theme of camp that year, and singing that always seems to lift the rafters. Those nights, it's like you get a small dose of what heaven will be like. Wednesday night's worship was as inspiring as the other nights had been. I was moved by the unity felt in the air that particular evening. But then something hit me like a Mack truck.

Have you ever had a moment when you were moving in one direction and something distracted you? It was a ninety-degree turn, abrupt and sudden. The song being sung at this moment was "Open the Eyes of My Heart." No instruments, just young voices longing to be changed by Jesus. I began weeping uncontrollably. What I had not acknowledged these past two days came into clear view during this song.

On Tuesday, God had sent a specific assignment at my request in prayer. The young girl seeking reconciliation with her youth minister had been my answer. The first wool fleece had been put out and was brought back sopping wet. Then today, Wednesday, God had sent the second of my specific requests on the deck of the mess hall at 2:00. I could not believe it had taken me two whole days to realize that God was answering my prayer, expanding my territory, reminding me that I was his and that his desire was to use me. He had not left me alone to ponder his inclusiveness of me in his work in the world.

Even as I had sat by the creek and wondered if I was too small or too weak to be any good to him, he had sent a message to me. That message said: Nothing is impossible for God! By surrendering, you gain everything. My prayer had been answered. My confidence was at an all-time high, because I had heard God's voice in my life. God had included me in his story all along. He was using me. He wants to use you as well.

So what's *your* prayer? Do you think your past will keep God from using you? Do you believe that you have no talent, no gift set, nothing admirable that God can use? Do you wish that God would listen to you in your moment of need? Are you hiding in a figurative winepress? What would it take for you to realize that God loves you and will use you? How is your prayer life? For what do you pray?

My hope for you is that you will let God open the eyes of your heart to see that, with his presence, you are bigger, smarter, better, more beautiful, more talented, and more courageous than you ever thought possible. Will you let him use you, despite what anyone else says? He's asking right now, "What's your sheepskin moment? How can I show you that you are my child?"

The story he is creating in this world is one where you are part of the story. Like Gideon (and me), stop hiding and start looking for the opportunities God is giving you to make a mark, to make a difference . . . to be a tupos.

Study Guide for Chapter Four: Experience

Read the text:

Judges 6:

The Israelites did evil in the LORD's sight. So the LORD handed them over to the Midianites for seven years. The Midianites were so cruel that the Israelites made hiding places for themselves in the mountains, caves, and strongholds. Whenever the Israelites planted their crops, marauders from Midian, Amalek, and the people of the east would attack Israel, camping in the land and destroying crops as far away as Gaza. They left the Israelites with nothing to eat, taking all the sheep, goats, cattle, and donkeys. These enemy hordes, coming with their livestock and tents, were as thick as locusts; they arrived on droves of camels too numerous to count. And they stayed until the land was stripped bare. So Israel was reduced to starvation by the Midianites. Then the Israelites cried out to the LORD for help.

When they cried out to the LORD because of Midian, the LORD sent a prophet to the Israelites. He said, "This is what the LORD, the God of Israel, says: I brought you up out of slavery in Egypt. I rescued you from the Egyptians and from all who oppressed you. I drove out your enemies and gave you their land. I told you, 'I am the LORD your God. You must not worship the gods of the Amorites, in whose land you now live.' But you have not listened to me."

Then the angel of the Lord came and sat beneath the great tree at Ophrah, which belonged to Joash of the clan of Abiezer. Gideon son of Joash was threshing wheat at the bottom of a winepress to hide the grain from the Midianites. The angel of the LORD appeared to him and said, "Mighty hero, the LORD is with you!"

"Sir," Gideon replied, "if the LORD is with us, why has all this happened to us? And where are all the miracles our ancestors told us about? Didn't they say, 'The LORD brought us up out of Egypt'? But now the LORD has abandoned us and handed us over to the Midianites."

Then the Lord turned to him and said, "Go with the strength you have, and rescue Israel from the Midianites. I am sending you!"

"But LORD," Gideon replied, "how can I rescue Israel? My clan is the weakest in the whole tribe of Manasseh, and I am the least in my entire family!"

The LORD said to him, "I will be with you. And you will destroy the Midianites as if you were fighting against one man." Gideon replied, "If you are truly going to help me, show me a sign to prove that it is really the LORD speaking to me. Don't go away until I come back and bring my offering to you." He answered, "I will stay here until you return."

Gideon hurried home. He cooked a young goat, and with a basket of flour he baked some bread without yeast. Then, carrying the meat in a basket and the broth in a pot, he brought them out and presented them to the angel, who was under the great tree.

The angel of God said to him, "Place the meat and the unleavened bread on this rock, and pour the broth over it." And Gideon did as he was told. Then the angel of the LORD touched the meat and bread with the tip of the staff in his hand, and fire flamed up from the rock and consumed all he had brought. And the angel of the LORD disappeared.

When Gideon realized that it was the angel of the Lord, he cried out, "Oh, Sovereign Lord, I'm doomed! I have seen the angel of the LORD face to face!"

"It is all right," the LORD replied. "Do not be afraid. You will not die." And Gideon built an altar to the LORD there and named it Yahweh-Shalom (which means "the LORD is peace"). The altar remains in Ophrah in the land of the clan of Abiezer to this day.

That night the LORD said to Gideon, "Take the second bull from your father's herd, the one that is seven years old. Pull down your father's altar to Baal, and cut down the Asherah pole standing beside it. Then build an altar to the LORD your God here on this hilltop sanctuary, laying the stones carefully. Sacrifice the bull as a burnt offering on the altar, using as fuel the wood of the Asherah pole you cut down."

So Gideon took ten of his servants and did as the LORD had commanded. But he did it at night because he was afraid of the other members of his father's household and the people of the town.

Early the next morning, as the people of the town began to stir, someone discovered that the altar of Baal had been broken down and that the Asherah pole beside it had been cut down. In their place a new altar had been built, and on it were the remains of the bull that had been sacrificed. The people said to each other, "Who did this?" And after asking around and making a careful search, they learned that it was Gideon, the son of Joash.

"Bring out your son," the men of the town demanded of Joash. "He must die for destroying the altar of Baal and for cutting down the Asherah pole."

But Joash shouted to the mob that confronted him, "Why are you defending Baal? Will you argue his case? Whoever pleads his case will be put to death by morning! If Baal truly is a god, let him defend himself and destroy the one who broke down his altar!" From then on Gideon was called Jerub-baal, which means, "Let Baal defend himself," because he broke down Baal's altar.

Soon afterward the armies of Midian, Amalek, and the people of the east formed an alliance against Israel and crossed the Jordan, camping in the valley of Jezreel. Then the Spirit of the LORD clothed Gideon with power. He blew a ram's horn as a call to arms, and the men of the clan of Abiezer came to him. He also sent messengers throughout Manasseh, Asher, Zebulun, and Naphtali, summoning their warriors, and all of them responded.

Then Gideon said to God, "If you are truly going to use me to rescue Israel as you promised, prove it to me in this way. I will put a wool fleece on the threshing floor tonight. If the fleece is wet with dew in the morning but the ground is dry, then I will know that you are going to help me rescue Israel as you promised." And that is just what happened. When Gideon got up early the next morning, he squeezed the fleece and wrung out a whole bowlful of water.

Then Gideon said to God, "Please don't be angry with me, but let me make one more request. Let me use the fleece for one more test. This time let the fleece remain dry while the ground around it is wet with dew." So that night God did as Gideon asked. The fleece was dry in the morning, but the ground was covered with dew.

Open:

Tell us about a time you felt God was not coming to your rescue. What encouraged you through that period of time?

Dig in:

1. When have you been given an encouraging word from God, but doubted it because of your circumstance? Who brought that word, or how was it delivered?

2. The New Testament reveals to us a loving and compassionate God. "God with us" is Jesus. He says, "If you have seen me, you've seen the Father" (see John 14:9). However, Judges 6:1 indicates God "handed them over." Does God hand over his people to chaotic and tragic ways? Explain.

3. Gideon tears down the altars to the false prophets. What idols need to be torn down in our culture today? Why? What might be the result of these idols remaining in place?

4. The New Testament is clear that each of us have been given talents and gifts to use for the glory of God. No matter how large or small we believe we are, we are called by God to live out his plan for us. What are some barriers you've discovered that make it difficult to fully live each day to God's glory?

5. What are ways our church can better encourage the use of everyone's gifts within our congregation?

6. Look around the room. Sometimes we're not sure what our calling or gift set might be. Allow time to tell others what you perceive their gifts to be.

CHAPTER FIVE

STORY:
YOU ARE PART OF SOMETHING BIGGER

S tory is a way to relive, retell, re-experience a moment in time. And anyone can tell a story. If you have children or grandchildren, you know. Think back to the occasion when you were ready to help that young child say what was on their mind. You have sat through the painstaking eternity of giving the time needed for a story to develop from those kids who are under five years of age, telling you exactly what their brother did to them in the backyard while you were not looking. Now don't get me wrong. It's cute and beautiful to interact in the lives of kids that you call your own. These are your kids and no amount of time is really ever wasted. You are giving them the attention needed to develop vocabulary, truth-telling, and the feeling of the presence of someone who truly cares for them.

Then there are moments (if you are married) where you begin to tell your story and your spouse begins to insert pieces into your story as he or she listens. I have been married for more than twenty-six years and I should be used to this by now. I am telling a story to my friends, or my sons, or my son's friends, and at the apex of my glorious oozing of the "facts," my wife says, "I don't remember it happening that way"; "No, this person was there, not the one you remember"; or "Nope! I'm pretty sure that's not the way that went down." You've been there before when at the end of your story, you're left with a feeling of, "Well, I thought that was exactly the way I remembered it all coming to pass." All the excitement was stolen from you by someone un-embellishing your story.

But then you've had the moments, the blessed assurance of how it all came to be, how you know it went down, how you are so firm in your understanding of the story nothing could sway you from how you are telling it, when you have gotten to tell the greatest story ever told.

God is a storyteller. His story is positively life-altering. I mean, the story of God is life-changing any way you slice it. Once you open yourself to who Jesus the Christ is and what he will do for you (see Romans 3:21–26), your life will never be the same. Once you know what Jesus did for you, you will want to position your life to do something for him. The excitement of your own saving in Jesus will change the way you live. The love Jesus offers you will create ripples of love in your life that extend to all those whose lives intersect with your own. You will want to let everyone know how truly great is our God. Peace and joy will reign over you and through you when you choose to follow Jesus and be his follower.

I have had the incredible blessing of taking several short-term mission trips all over the world with groups of teenagers and their chaperones. As a youth pastor, my habit was to ask the graduating senior high class if they would like to go do mission work somewhere or just go on a fun trip. Only two of those graduating classes said "only fun," while all the others said, "Let's go be a part of someone's story in the world. Let's be a part of infusing their story with the ultimate story of Jesus."

We have had the true blessing of assisting churches and people in Los Angeles, Manhattan, New York, Lyon, France, Jamaica, Kenya, Vanuatu (islands in the South Pacific), Cameroon, West Africa, Honduras, and the little-known country of Croatia on the Adriatic Sea between central and southeast Europe. Croatia is a richly beautiful country full of delightful people who have their own incredible story.

The forerunners of modern Croats arrived in the area to begin settling present-day Croatia in the early part of the seventh century AD. They evolved into a proud people and organized themselves into two duchies by the ninth century, retaining their sovereignty for two centuries. Fast-forward one thousand years to the mass carnage that was World War I (1914–1918). In the European chaos that reigned after that great and bloody war, Croatia was included in the unrecognized State of Slovenes, Croats, and Serbs, which had seceded from Austria-Hungary and ultimately became the country of Yugoslavia. The state of Croatia was lost in the melting pot of multiethnic groups and socialism of Yugoslavia after World War I.

But right on the heels of World War I, a new world war broke out, fueled by Germany's resentment of the treaties signed at the end of the First World War. Using these emotions and a bleak economy, the Nazi party rose to lead Germany.

During the territory-grabbing establishment of Nazi Germany and World War II (1939–1945), socialist Croatia became a puppet state for Nazi Germany and fascist Italy. The chief Allied powers of England, France, China, Russia, and the US defeated the Axis powers of Germany, Italy, and Japan, finishing the world war in 1945. A total of fifty-five million people lost their lives.

After World War II was over, six socialist republics, controlled by the Soviet Union, emerged in Yugoslavia: Bosnia and

Herzegovina, Croatia, Macedonia (the same place the apostle Paul went to do mission work in Acts 20), Montenegro, Serbia, and Slovenia. As a people group longing to tell its own story and history, Croatia began its hope for independence.

So in June 1991 Croatia declared its independence, after years of nationalistic demonstrations. A desire to be their own governing people, to tell their story in a more personal way, led to their hope for independence out of the melting pot of post-Yugoslavia. The Croatian civil war of independence was fought successfully for four years. Now Croatia is once again a sovereign nation, a proud people with an honored heritage. It is governed by a parliamentary system by their own elected people. Today, their story is being told in ways that have been hampered by past regimes and governments.

Croatians have always had a close tie to God's story as seen through the generations. In their new republic created after their civil war in 1992, freedom of religion became the right of every person, supported by their constitution for those who live in Croatia.

Croatia has no official religion but religious loyalties break down roughly like this: Roman Catholic makes up 87%, followed by Eastern Orthodox making up 5%, followed by Islamic adherents by 1.5%, followed by Protestantism and other Christian groups at 1%. Of course in our current postmodern culture, there are always the ever-increasing "nones"—citizens who claim no religion (about 5%). The same poll asked, "Is religion an important part of your daily life?" While 70% answered "yes," only 24% attend religious services on a regular basis.[1] Almost sounds like the good ol' USA.

In 2001, I lived in Oklahoma. The church where I worked had a connection with Ivan, a Croatian native missionary in Zapresic, a suburb of the Croatian capital of Zagreb. I began talking with

Ivan and made plans to take a short-term mission team to Zapresic to help with constructing some of their new church building, and to help tell the greatest story ever told in the way of the church's *first-ever* Vacation Bible School for their children.

Our team (Beverly, Stephen, Alicia, Marissa, Chris, Robin, and me) began meeting together in the spring of 2001 to discuss how the VBS would be arranged, what stories we would tell, what materials we might need to carry, and who would be in charge of what stations for the kids. It was exciting as the countdown reached zero and we boarded our airplane, bound for this little beautiful country on the Adriatic Sea. Many of us held tension and anxiety about the trip.

Think for a moment: When have you been outside your comfort zone? What trips have you been a part of where you spent your hard-earned money to do something that was not very "vacation-y" but more focused on other people? When have the lives of other people been more important than your own? When have you given up your time, gift set, or material possessions so that other people could hear the story that would change their entire lives—and the next?

If you are having trouble answering these questions, let me encourage you as a follower of Jesus of Nazareth, Jesus' words are golden. If you feel like you need purpose, validation, direction, intentionality, or a way to feel like you have made a difference in this world, then follow Jesus and discover ways to tell his story. It's a story of hope and promise as old as time. Jesus reminds his disciples (and us) in Matthew 10:39, "If you cling to your life, you will lose it; but if you give up your life for me, you will find it."

So, the seven of us boarded our plane, ready to lose our lives to tell the exciting story of Jesus. We arrived in Zagreb and were picked up at the airport by Ivan, who transported us to several houses where we would live for the week. Unfortunately, upon arrival Ivan let us know that the building project at church was at a standstill, so all we could do was some cleanup and move materials from one location to another. We were happy to do that, but a little bummed that we couldn't do more. However, the sun came up on Sunday morning, and brought with it the launch of VBS.

In moments when I travel abroad and visit a church outside the United States, it seems customary to allow the visiting pastor to preach. Croatia was no different, and I was excited to deliver the Sunday morning message, with the help of a local interpreter.

I do not know how many of you have ever spoken a sentence at a time and waited for someone else to explain what you said. I would imagine the experience would be similar to your millennial fifteen-year-old son explaining how to use Instagram to your ninety-nine-year-old grandma. It would be lethargic, messy, slow, repetitive, confusing, frustrating . . . you get the idea. One would get a small feeling of how it must have been at the Tower of Babel in Genesis 11 when God created multiple languages to prevent humankind from making any progress on building their "stairway to heaven." It's an interesting story.

Tower of Babel moment . . . talk about confusion. I recently was in Honduras where I was asked to preach for the Spanish-speaking congregation. The story I used was one most all followers of Christ know from Matthew 14 about Jesus and Peter walking on the water.

Have you ever had a moment when you thought what you were doing was so good and meant to glorify God only to feel the powers of Hell had come together to stop your plan? About five minutes before I got up to preach, the heavens opened up to unleash a torrential downpour of rain. Did I mention the church building had a tin roof in which we were gathered? Can you say the word "deafening"? On top of the deluge, my interpreter did not show up, so I had to use someone from the audience who was not used to interpreting for a preacher (although she did a great job). On top of that, the power went out, which left me no microphone to pitch my voice above the storm. At times, you may feel that way as well as you try to make your mark telling the story of Jesus in the best way you know how. There are moments you use others' words to speak the message of Jesus because you don't know the language, which is what happened that Sunday morning in Croatia.

As I was preaching that morning in Zapresic, having difficulty getting any traction because of the verbal ping-pong match between me and my interpreter, I noticed two boys running across the seats on the back row, grabbing purses, picking up things that did not belong to them, taking just about anything that was not nailed down. It was as if they had not gotten the memo about how one should act while in church, especially when a guest preacher is doing his best to keep anyone's attention.

I finally managed to preach through all the distraction, while our crew did their best to corral these two young boys. The sermon ended with us saying goodbye to the local attendees, and Ivan taking us to lunch.

Ivan explained over lunch who these boys were, and their background. The Croatian word he used is *cigan;* the more common word is "gypsy." They are known worldwide as Romani (not to be confused with Romanian). These people are traditionally a nomadic ethnic group originating from the northern points of the Indian continent, and have a rich traditional history of music, dancing, and language. Their nomadic tendencies make them great foragers—hence these boys' ability, on a Sunday morning, to pick up anything that wasn't being held by a person. It was actually funny watching all the Americans faced with two small boys who they couldn't control. It was funny because I was preaching and didn't have to try to contain them as my other six compadres did. After lunch, we rested and talked about the launch that evening of the first-ever VBS at the Zapresic Church.

It was beautiful that first night. Families were lined up to get the kids registered. Once we welcomed everyone and got started, all the parents stood at the back to see what a VBS looked like. No one had ever singled out their children to pour the story of Jesus into, in a way kids could fully understand and appreciate. The songs were age-appropriate; the activities were fun and attention-grabbing. The Bible story was told in a way that an adolescent, even one speaking another language, could grasp and follow (with the aid of an interpreter, of course).

Mothers were smiling ear to ear to see their children embraced, loved on, lifted up, played with, and encouraged on their journey in the story of Jesus. Even the gypsy kids seemed to enjoy themselves, albeit at a much faster pace. The whole three-day VBS went off without a hitch. The local kids loved on us and we loved them back. We gained insight into the lives of brothers and sisters in Christ that we didn't know prior to traveling to Croatia. All of us left with a better sense of commitment in our lives, a better vision of the how big the world truly is, and a healthier awareness of our purpose in God's story.

I am currently reading through the story of the Bible this year, using a social media app. I have challenged our church to do this with me. It is always fascinating to me how much I uncover in the Bible although I've read it many times. I'll read through a pericope (passage), and then reread the same text because I discovered something I had not seen before in my reading. Have you ever done that? Has something ever jumped off the page that has been there, but you never saw it before? It always makes me ask myself, "What else have I not seen before?"

As I read through Abram and Sarai's story about leaving their country, their family and their friends in Genesis 12, I'm reminded that Abram was a nomad as well . . . like those boys, the gypsies, at our VBS. They came to listen to the story of God (and have some fun). Nomadic Abram listened to God's voice, as his story began to unfold in the story of God. We are all nomads if you think about it, wandering through this world trying to discover our purpose.

The apostle Peter quotes the prophet Hosea from the Hebrew Bible and says in 1 Peter 2:10, "Once you had no identity as a people; now you are God's people. Once you received no mercy; now you have received God's mercy." Peter goes on to call followers of Jesus "temporary residents and foreigners" in this world" (v. 11). Peter calls us nomads. We are just passing through. And like our friends, the gypsy boys, we end up trying to pick up and take everything that's not nailed down in this life. We believe a particular thing, (_____—fill in the blank with the thing you believe will save the day, make you feel better, get you high enough to look down on others, feel accomplished, have control) will indeed make us fulfill our purpose and give us a satisfied life.

But remember, Jesus told us that if we try to hang onto this life, we end up losing it. If we truly want purpose, fulfillment, satisfaction, joy, a smile in this life, we have to let go of all the things we are trying to "gypsy" and lean into God's story. We have to let go of that which we have a death-hold on and let God's story grasp us. We will have to let go of the story we are trying to build and let God's story build us. What we find, if we sit long enough and listen, is that our very character is actually in the story. God has written us in. He's waiting for us to lean forward into his story, and to take the more active role as nomads who are headed home.

So, what is causing your anxiousness and fidgety spirit? Are you tired of being the gypsy? What makes you unable to sit still and listen to God? What would occur if you realized you were actually in the story of God? How would you reorient your life, knowing God wants you in his story? What magnificent moment would ensue in your life if you simply leaned into the story God is telling right now in our world?

You and I have been created in the image of God. God is the master storyteller, and you are created in his image. That means you are a storyteller as well. What story are you telling with your life? Is that script working? Don't you think it's time to stop collecting things and controlling things?

In the back of this book, write down the three things that you are ready to let go of in order to better hear the story of God in your life. Beside each item, write what person in your life will better help you accomplish laying that thing down. God is so ready to use you in his story. Are you ready for your story to be positively, overwhelmingly, graciously astounded by the tidal wave of love that is God? Are you ready to have the quieted peace in your life that you have been missing all these years? Could you possibly be prepared to embrace all the hugging and kissing your soul has been longing for from your Creator?

Yeah . . . me too!

Study Guide for Chapter Five: Story

Read the text:

Genesis 12:1–9:

The LORD had said to Abram, "Leave your native country, your relatives, and your father's family, and go to the land that I will show you. I will make you into a great nation. I will bless you and make you famous, and you will be a blessing to others. I will bless those who bless you and curse those who treat you with contempt. All the families on earth will be blessed through you."

So Abram departed as the LORD had instructed, and Lot went with him. Abram was seventy-five years old when he left Haran. He took his wife, Sarai, his nephew Lot, and all his wealth—his livestock and all the people he had taken into his household at Haran—and headed for the land of Canaan. When they arrived in Canaan, Abram traveled through the land as far as Shechem. There he set up camp beside the oak of Moreh. At that time, the area was inhabited by Canaanites.

Then the LORD appeared to Abram and said, "I will give this land to your descendants." And Abram built an altar there and dedicated it to the LORD, who had appeared to him. After that, Abram traveled south and set up camp in the hill country, with Bethel to the west and Ai to the east. There he built another altar and dedicated it to the Lord, and he worshiped the Lord. Then Abram continued traveling south by stages toward the Negev.

Open:

What is the biggest, most exciting gift you have ever received? Who gave it to you? How did you feel? What ended up happening to the gift?

Dig in:

1. Where have you lived the longest? Do you feel you have roots there? How sentimental is that place to you? Knowing all that, how do you believe Abram felt when he left his roots, following God's guidance?

2. God promised to make Abram a blessing to others. In what ways, both immediately in Abram's life and in his future, do you see Abram being a blessing?

3. Abram did not leave his home alone. He had close family around him that went as well. How did they contribute to helping Abram be a blessing for God? In what ways are they also a part of the blessing?

4. Abram traveled in community. What should this tell us about our spiritual journey as we move through this life? How important is it to not travel alone?

5. As followers of Christ, we're called to listen to God's leading and follow. What are some ways you have listened to the call of God in your life? How has that made a difference in your outcomes?

6. What would it take for you to fully submit to God's calling, realizing we are commanded in Mark 12:30–31 to follow him with all our heart, soul, mind, and strength? What does that mean to you?

7. Abram built an altar at the end of his journey. He worshiped God. How is listening to God's call worship? What does that look like, as it plays out in our everyday life?

8. What altars in our lives interfere with us truly worshiping God and following his lead? How do we overcome those

distractions in order to fully follow God wherever he is leading us?

9. In what ways can our congregation better listen to God? What are some practices or disciplines our church should incorporate in order to better hear the voice of God?

CHAPTER SIX

LOST:

JESUS IS THERE—EVEN WHEN
THE LIGHTS ARE OUT

*W*hen I was a youth minister in central Oklahoma, I loved hanging with the teens in my youth group. They were a ton of fun and we had many adventures together. One of those adventures happened every year in the month of May. Every graduating class of seniors got to choose a trip. We could go on a mission trip. You just read about one of those incredible trips we took to Croatia. We could just go have some fun somewhere. Or we could do a combination.

In 2005 I had three seniors in the group, but only one was really active: Wyatt Wilson. I was blessed to baptize him and later marry him and his wife, Katie. He protects our country right now as a Marine officer. I am appreciative of Wyatt's service and sacrifice. As you know, good friends are often created by life experiences and I consider him a good friend.

I asked Wyatt mid-spring what he might like to do on his senior trip; I was open to anything. I should have considered that Wyatt was one tough dude who worked out and I . . . was not. But Wyatt said, "Let's go hike a couple of fourteeners."

In regular, lay language, he wanted to hike some 14,000-foot mountains in Colorado.

If you have ever ridden a roller coaster, you know there is a moment when they put down the arm bar. You hear it "click." That's the point of no return—when you are going on this ride whether you want to or not. This is where I found myself with Wyatt and our trip to hike a couple of real mountains.

The day after his high school graduation, Wyatt and I jumped into the car and drove westward, toward the Rocky Mountains and Denver, Colorado. Once we arrived in Denver, we checked into our hotel and drove immediately to REI. After all, we were a couple of guys from Oklahoma. What did we know about climbing mountains? We thought we could buy some cool gear and get great advice from the folks at REI about where to go and climb.

Once at REI, we looked at water filters, hiking shoes, day-packs, trail maps and hiking books. While in the trail map area of the store, we began talking to a male employee. He had seen us looking at trail maps and books about where to go and climb, so he came over to offer his advice. He took one look at us and decided he knew just where to send us; he said we looked fit and able to do the mountain trails on Mount Evans and Mount Bierstadt. Well, we bought into his confidence in us. We bought the trail book and took off to get some rest at the hotel before heading out early the next morning. We were pumped and excited.

The alarm went off at 4:00 a.m. We awoke to the "beep . . . beep . . . beep" and our adrenaline kicked in as we headed out the door to the car. After two hours of driving west of Denver, Wyatt and I discovered the pass in the mountain while driving the 2003 black Sequoia that I still drive today. We pulled over to the side of the road, put two bottles of water in our daypacks, a few light snacks and began our journey.

I walked a few hundred feet from the SUV to the edge of the canyon. We soaked in the beauty of the postcard picture that lay in front of us. After a few moments breathing in the panoramic view, we took our first steps toward the canyon floor.

If you've ever seen the National Mall in Washington, DC in a movie or in a picture, you cannot fathom how long and large that space is until you visit there and walk it yourself. It will fool you. You'd better pack a lunch. The same is true of the mountains in Colorado. As we started down the pass toward the canyon floor, it seemed like it was right there, an arm's length away, a stone's throw. After slipping on shale and climbing over huge boulders, working hard to keep balance, we finally reached the bottom two hours after our start. That much work requires rest and water. Did I mention that we were from Oklahoma, where oxygen is abundant? To say the least, we were winded.

After pausing again to catch our breath, Wyatt and I started across the canyon floor, dodging mountain goat dung and underground springs. Again, what seemed like a stroll from the couch to the kitchen fridge turned into another two- or three-hour walk, until we finally reached the other mountain where the real climbing began (yes, we really had not climbed anything yet!). We sat and rested for several minutes to get our wits about us.

Wyatt pulled me onto my feet and urged me onward, up the side of these huge boulders, carefully placing our hands and feet in the crevices in order to push our way up the side of the other mountainside. After hours of climbing, sliding, catching our breath, avoiding goat poop, and encouraging each other onward, we reached the crest of Mount Bierstadt, where we wrote our names in the summit register placed at the top of the mountain by the National Park Service.

By the time we summited Bierstadt, Wyatt and I were exhausted, out of breath, spent, tired, lightheaded and, oh, out of water. After sitting for just a moment, we decided to get back to the Sequoia, since it was already late afternoon. We started our descent into the valley, making a decision to take a "short cut" across the valley and to the gorge where, at the top, our vehicle and more water awaited. However, on our way down, it began to snow on us! Neither of us had brought any cold-weather gear because, remember, it was supposed to be a quick trip over to the other side and back. With no water, no cold weather gear, and it now snowing, Wyatt and I hastened our trip across the valley floor and over to the gorge that we needed to climb to get to our vehicle.

At the bottom of the gorge we needed to climb to get to our vehicle and water, I realized I had failed to look behind me in our original descent. There were actually four gorges in front of me—and they all looked the same. At the top of one of them was our salvation. But we now had additional issues. The oxygen had seemingly been vacuumed out of the canyon. Our breathing was deeply labored, we had cotton mouth, and we continued to be lightheaded.

Wyatt and I were so spent, so exhausted, that we had to lie down on our belly and "army crawl." We were so dehydrated. We had not had any water in hours. We weren't sweating any-more. It was snowing on us. We could not breathe. We would literally crawl twenty-five feet and have to wait a few minutes to catch our breath. We were so exhausted that we no longer cared about the goat poop that we found our faces in. A state of panic set in as darkness was coming on. Wyatt told me to tell Katie that he loved her. I told him to tell Robin I was sorry I ate her school lunch that was left in the fridge two weeks ago. We both encouraged each other to keep going at all costs. I told him it was Tuesday and it would be Saturday before anyone knew we were missing. I heard a distant wolf howl. I thought I felt Sasquatch watching us. We had to get out of the deep, dark canyon tonight. So we started up the first gorge, slowly . . . painfully.

As I began to pull my way up, I began to notice piles of snow on the side of the gorge. I hadn't noticed that snow coming down. I began to second-guess myself. Do I take a chance and keep going? Or do I take a chance and go back down to try a different route? In a state of drained and weakened confusion, something told me to go back down, so I did.

We moved over to the very next gorge, full of boulders and loose rocks, and began climbing. Wyatt was right there with me, each of us supporting and encouraging the other. But something interesting happened to me that Wyatt did not, could not see as we ascended the second gorge. As I was crawling on the ground upward, I lifted my eyes up about one hundred yards in front of me.

I don't know if you've ever had a moment when you saw something in disbelief, as real as the hand in front of your face. You see it, rub your eyes, shake the cobwebs out of your head, and refocus your eyes to better see what you thought you saw. It's like that Christmas morning as a kid when you arose early at the crack of dawn to discover that Santa brought you *everything* on your list! Yeah, that kind of disbelief.

You see, as I looked up the gorge, I saw, in broad daylight, my oldest son Tanner coming through a door. The door was not attached to anything. He closed the door and began walking downhill toward me. I looked at Wyatt and asked if he could see what I was seeing. He had no idea what I was talking about. I turned from Wyatt and looked again. Tanner was still walking toward me, all the while smiling his big, beautiful smile. He has his thumb out, as if hitchhiking, but using it to point up the gorge as if to say, "This is the way you need to go, dad. I'm helping you out." I looked at Wyatt again but when I turned a second time, my vision of Tanner was gone. Knowing how helpful Tanner has always been to me, I followed his thumb and my gut.

Putting one foot in front of the other, we pulled ourselves up with arms that felt like spaghetti. Slowly we reached the top of that gorge. I pulled myself over the final ledge, reaching back to extend a hand to my good friend Wyatt, and wouldn't you know it—at the top was our vehicle, and in it was water!

Wyatt and I crawled to the vehicle and drank our fill of water, lying in the grass as we drank. Cars would slow down on the road and ask if we were doing okay; we'd simply give them a thumb raised high in the air. We had planned on tenting on the mountain, but after catching our breaths we slid into the Sequoia and headed down the mountain, driving all the way to Denver and a comfortable hotel room.

Wyatt and I learned some things on that trip. One is that preparedness pays off. Being ready for an event, a life moment, a conversation, cannot be underestimated. But something else was reaffirmed that day: Although unseen at times, God is ever-present. Protecting, guiding, steering, providing.

Tell the truth; you've had moments like that in life. Moments when you couldn't see clearly. Moments when you couldn't make out which way to go because the proverbial rug had been yanked out from under your feet. I can only imagine what Jesus' disciples must have felt like after that Passover weekend when

Jesus was killed and his body had been hurriedly placed in a borrowed tomb carved out of the side of a hill. What panic they must have felt! Imagine the anxiety each follower had welling up deep inside his or her gut. What do we do now? Where do we go from here?

In Luke 24, we read the story about a couple on the morning Jesus was resurrected, which can act as a metaphor of our spiritual life at times. A town called Emmaus sits about seven miles from Jerusalem. I believe our pair was a married couple who lived in Emmaus, and who had been in Jerusalem for the Passover festivities. We don't know how long they had been Jesus' followers, but based on their conversation they knew Jesus well. Because of the Jewish rules for Passover and Sabbath, the couple couldn't walk home from Jerusalem on Saturday; it was too far for what the Jewish Law permitted. So, first light on Sunday morning, they began their journey back to the old homestead, talking about the weekend and things going on in life. Were the two of them just talking about the big game or maybe trading in the old donkey for a new one or maybe how Cleopas needed to stop watching football on the weekend and fix the hole in the roof? No! Truth is, they were not talking about ordinary stuff. They were discussing the last days and hours of Jesus of Nazareth.

For centuries, there had been prophecies written in the Hebrew text about a Messiah (which means "Anointed One" in Hebrew), a redeemer, a rescuer sent from God. This couple, their parents, grandparents, and great-grandparents would have known these stories and prophecies and would have been excitedly awaiting the Messiah to come rescue all of Israel. In their lifetimes, they would have been hoping, praying, dreaming, expecting this person from God to show up—when suddenly,

Jesus from Nazareth seemed to fit everything they had been taught and imagined.

Jesus' teaching was incredible—almost like he'd written the material from which he was instructing and preaching. His style of teaching challenged the current status quo and the religious elite of the day. The emotional connection he felt with regular people, like you and me, could almost be held in your hand. The compassion he felt for those physically and emotionally hurting was evident in the time he took with each miracle he performed to get people back on their feet and functioning in a society that had sidelined them because of their deficiencies. This couple had asked, "Could he be the one?" At some point, they believed it, and began to follow this man from Nazareth—this rescuer, this purveyor of good news.

Except, three days earlier, the Romans in Jerusalem had crucified Jesus of Nazareth. All their hopes and dreams were gone in a moment. They were looking at their lives and saying, "Our lives are not going the way we thought or hoped they would. It's not the path we'd imagined for us."

The reality is, many of us are in a similar season as this distraught couple on the road to Emmaus. We look at our lives and wish things were different. We just want to be parents but for some reason, we cannot conceive. We finally graduated from college and cannot seem to find the job we were promised, yet have all this college debt. We thought we would be celebrating an anniversary, but now we are simply fighting over who gets the sofa and chair. We had hoped to retire, but unforeseen market events took half our savings. We had hoped to be enjoying life, but right now I'm fighting cancer. In the chaos of the walk home, you are confused, saddened, your heart is heavy with unanswered questions.

Have you ever had the answer right in front of you, but then not see it? Have you ever said that age-old saying, "If it'd been a snake, it would have bit me"?

I love the movie *National Lampoon's Christmas Vacation*, starring Chevy Chase. There's a scene where he's put a bazillion Christmas lights on his house, but he can't get them to come on. He's got the extension cords plugged in a room off the garage, not realizing the switch by the outlet must be turned on in order for the cords to get juice. They go back and forth in the movie to the garage room, unplugging cords and plugging them back in, turning the switch on the room to see what they are doing. It is a comedy of errors but all the while, the answer is right in front of them and they don't see it.

In our story on the road to Emmaus, Jesus begins walking with this couple—only they don't recognize him. Can you imagine Jesus' excitement? The very Jesus they are talking about begins the journey to Emmaus with them. And Jesus says to them, "What are you talking about?" I can only envision what Jesus had to do in order not to smile ear to ear. This couple doesn't realize that right in front of them is the King of kings, the risen Savior, the Rabbi whom they have been following and thought was dead. Jesus is thinking, "You don't see me yet, but the truth is right here in front of you." The couple, like so many of us, are hurting, confused, demoralized, sad, alone, afraid—when life-changing truth is right in front of us!

Some of you are in a season of "hoped-for." You woke up one morning to realize the life you hoped for, the story of you, the way you thought it was going to be, is not going to come to fruition. That's where this Emmaus couple found themselves. They were hopeless when Eternal Hope was walking with them.

Sometimes it's hard to see God in your present situation. You wonder if he cares. You wonder if he's forgotten you. You wonder if you are praying hard enough. You wonder if he's letting you do this one alone.

However, when you look in life's rearview mirror, you can see how God has been present and walked with you all along. They say hindsight is 20/20. So many times in our spiritual journey, that is so true. We look behind us in our story to discover that every single time we thought we were alone, God was there in the journey as well. God was with me when I felt lonely, in despair, in the financial crisis, in my loss, in my grief, in the night of life, lost in the mountains of life. For our Emmaus couple, it is a dark moment, but true to Jesus' teaching, they are hospitable and invite this stranger into their home for the night.

The three of them sit down for a meal. I find it interesting that Jesus, not the host, picks up the bread to break it and bless the meal. Breaking bread and blessing. Sounds familiar, doesn't it? That Friday night with the disciples in the Upper Room. Jesus did the same thing during the Passover meal. Based on Jewish traditions alone, we know that more than the twelve disciples were in that Upper Room. What if our Emmaus couple had been present at that Passover meal? What if they had heard Jesus say the prayer over the bread and watered wine, reminding all of them that this symbolism had a different meaning now? It now symbolized Jesus, the Anointed One of God—his broken body and shed blood for a new way of living. And now, this couple is watching this reenacted for them at their own dining room table!

The text in Luke tells us that upon Jesus breaking the bread, the couple's eyes were opened. They could see Jesus for who he really was—the redeemer, the rescuer, the Savior, Emmanuel,

God with us, the provider and protector. And in our life, we too can believe and rest assured that even in difficult moments— when we think God is nowhere near—if we open our eyes, we may find that he's never left us. In fact, he's been traveling with us the entire time.

Study Guide for Chapter Six: Lost

Read the text:

Luke 24:13–32:

That same day two of Jesus' followers were walking to the village of Emmaus, seven miles from Jerusalem. As they walked along they were talking about everything that had happened. As they talked and discussed these things, Jesus himself suddenly came and began walking with them. But God kept them from recognizing him. He asked them, "What are you discussing so intently as you walk along?"

They stopped short, sadness written across their faces. Then one of them, Cleopas, replied, "You must be the only person in Jerusalem who hasn't heard about all the things that have happened there the last few days."

"What things?" Jesus asked.

"The things that happened to Jesus, the man from Nazareth," they said. "He was a prophet who did powerful miracles, and he was a mighty teacher in the eyes of God and all the people. But our leading priests and other religious leaders handed him over to be condemned to death, and they crucified him. We had hoped he was the Messiah who had come to rescue Israel. This all happened three days ago.

"Then some women from our group of his followers were at his tomb early this morning, and they came back with an amazing report. They said his body was missing, and they had seen angels who told them Jesus is alive! Some of our men ran out to see, and sure enough, his body was gone, just as the women had said." Then Jesus said to them, "You foolish people! You find it so hard to believe all that the prophets wrote in the

Scriptures. Wasn't it clearly predicted that the Messiah would have to suffer all these things before entering his glory?" Then Jesus took them through the writings of Moses and all the prophets, explaining from all the Scriptures the things concerning himself.

By this time they were nearing Emmaus and the end of their journey. Jesus acted as if he were going on, but they begged him, "Stay the night with us, since it is getting late." So he went home with them. As they sat down to eat, he took the bread and blessed it. Then he broke it and gave it to them. Suddenly, their eyes were opened, and they recognized him. And at that moment he disappeared!

They said to each other, "Didn't our hearts burn within us as he talked with us on the road and explained the Scriptures to us?"

Open:

Talk about a time when you were lost and didn't know which way to go or what to do. Who was with you? Why was that an asset or a disadvantage?

Dig in:

1. Emmaus is only seven miles from Jerusalem. But it was the Passover, which meant this couple could not have walked home on Saturday. It's very possible that these followers of Jesus were in the Upper Room with Jesus and the other disciples to celebrate this Jewish festival. Read John 14:1–14. How would this dialogue have been a blessing for this couple? What would they have thought about as Jesus revealed himself in their house?

2. Jesus is walking with them, and they don't know who he is. That seems odd. What do you believe is going on

here as they travel? Is he really unrecognizable? Are there moments in our own story where we don't realize Jesus is actually with us? How do we recognize him?

3. The couple revealed later in the story that as Jesus talked to them about prophecy and Scripture, they were "lit up." How do you feel when you read God's Word? Confused? Worried? Confident? Assured? Longing for more? Explain.

4. In their misunderstanding of teaching and text, Jesus calls the two "foolish." Have there been times in your life when Jesus revealed himself to you, and you felt foolish because of disbelief or lack of commitment? Describe how you felt, and how Jesus pulled you back into his story.

5. At the end of the journey, the couple invites Jesus into their home and they sit down for a meal. How important is it to be hospitable in our Christian walk? Why? What are things we can do to be more hospitable?

6. Describe ways you feel you've invited Jesus into your home. Maybe you've observed other fellow Christians who do this well. What are ways they have invited Jesus into their home?

7. Describe ways our church can become more hospitable to our community. How can we love our neighbor as a church with all our heart, soul, mind, and strength?

LOVE WITH ALL YOUR LOGIC (MIND)

"Fix your thoughts on what is true, and honorable,
and right, and pure, and lovely, and admirable.
Think about things that are excellent and
worthy of praise."

~Philippians 4:8

"Character is higher than intellect. A great soul will
be strong to live as well as think."

~Ralph Waldo Emerson,
American essayist

"It is not enough to have a good mind, the main
thing is to use it well."

~Rene Descartes,
Discourse on Method

Mark 12:30

"Love the LORD your God with all your . . .
mind (logic)"

CHAPTER SEVEN

SET:
THE AGE OF MEMORY

*L*earning everything you need to know on a test *and* committing it to memory is not an easy task. For example, it could take long, agonizing, tiring hours to memorize all the bones of the body; know what the capitals are of each state of our union; or, out of all the algebraic formulas available, correctly determine that this is the place where you use the quadratic formula.

I must confess, I have found it difficult to put in my memory bank all the things I need to know along life's way. What I have discovered is that if you do want to really know something—I mean know it inside and out, to be set in it, to know it like it's becoming part of your breathing where you don't even think about it—you have to spend a great deal of time with that particular item, thing, person, hobby, or book. It must become part of you and your life. It must be set within you.

When we were missionaries in Kumba, Cameroon, we committed to two full years of living there between 1975–1977. When I say "we," what I mean is that my dad did, and that meant we had to go as well. When one is in first and second grade, one doesn't get a whole lot of say where one lives. That's where I was in 1975.

Africa was a great adventure. We enjoyed the blessing of immersing ourselves in another culture, making new friends, and owning pets we could not own in the United States.

My dad is an advocate for learning and applying the wisdom of the Bible. So am I. He engrained early in me that the Bible was not to be taken lightly. If one is a God-lover, then the Bible should be followed. He taught me to have a high level of respect for the Bible from a young age. I do believe the Bible is a blueprint for life. I believe by using multiple lenses, one can see how God has called us to live life in the most abundant way possible. Those lenses include reading Scripture for what it is— understanding the writer and the recipient; understanding and embracing the cultural norms when it was written; considering the words used, and discerning the language and style of writing. Once you put all that together, one can make a head-and-heart decision as to what God is calling us to do. God wants what is best for his creation (us), doesn't he? Your best version of yourself can come to life by following God's calling as it is revealed in God's Word. After all, Jesus said that he'd come to give us life and to give us life to the fullest (John 10:10).

I think most people look at the Bible as a rulebook, a book that makes their life miserable. I should know. I was one of those people early in my adult life. Initially, I had decided that I knew me better than God did, so I was going to make the decisions for my life. If you've read the earlier chapters in this book, you saw where that got me: absolutely nowhere, except in the hole I was digging for myself.

But as I was digging that hole in my early twenties, on my mind constantly were God's healing words for me and my life.

And do you know when I really learned the importance of those God-words? In Africa, because my dad thought it was important. I have to say here: Thank you, Dad, for loving me enough to share your tenacity for learning God's words and making sure I did as well.

One thing I remember doing with my dad while in Africa was a study through the book of the Acts of the Apostles. Acts is the fifth letter in the New Testament part of the Bible; it was written by Luke (who also wrote the Gospel of Luke). This is the same Luke who was a doctor and traveled with Paul on his missionary journeys to plant churches, so people would know who Jesus was and is and could be to those who embraced him. It was Luke, who was a physician by trade, who traveled with the apostle Paul on his missionary journey, who wrote the letter of the Acts of the Apostles and what incredible things the early church experienced as it was first born into the world some two thousand years ago.

As we studied Acts, Dad would read through a pericope (passage) of the letter and discuss what had just happened in the early church. After every chapter, we talked about, studied on, immersed ourselves in, discussed *how* we were going to remember this chapter. What words, what mnemonic word phrases, were we going to use to remember that particular chapter, in order to recall the story Luke wrote?

So for instance, in Acts 1, we find Jesus and his disciples having a discussion. Jesus has been resurrected several weeks now. On different occasions, Jesus has been speaking with different groups of followers in different locations on different days. Jesus is encouraging his followers to be faithful, to stay in the area, and to tell the story of Good News to the entire world. Just after Jesus' affirmation on the Mount of Olives, he ascends to heaven because his work on earth was done. He had done everything the Bible ever said he would do, and now all of creation has the opportunity to be a part of his unifying story. So for us, we remembered Acts 1 as "Ascension" because Jesus ascended back to heaven leaving the kickoff of the church to his human followers—which was an incredibly risky move if you really consider how we are as humans. Certainly another story for another time.

Dad walked through the entire letter of Acts, pericope by pericope, chapter by chapter. We spent weeks discovering, learning, and being encouraged by the incredible things the early church had done. So, to this day, when someone asks, "Where were the first deacons in the church?" I immediately recall Acts 6 because we named it "Seven Men Chosen."

One of the blessings of living in Africa was that we didn't have many of the distractions Americans do today. We had no television for two years! My grandmother would record my favorite show, *Scooby Doo,* on cassette tape; thus, my two younger brothers and I would listen to that show instead of watch it.

Cell phones had not been invented, nor the Internet, so there was no social media or instant news (I know what you Millennials are thinking, "How did we survive?"). While all these things today create for us a sense of security, being in the know, and having community, those same things can distract us from discovering completely the fullness of life God wants to give his creation. Our current modern inventions are not bad things. But they can create distraction from what really matters.

Take Peter, the fisherman, the disciple and super-emotional follower of Jesus, who became the leader of the church in Jerusalem. He appears to be writing in 1 Peter to the house churches in the northern part of Asia Minor (present-day Turkey) in about 60 AD. Peter encourages those churches, and us today, "Worship Christ as Lord of your life. And if someone asks about your Christian hope, always be ready to explain it. But do this in a gentle and respectful way. Keep your conscience clear" (1 Peter 3:15–16).

In order to know how to worship Christ as Lord of your life, it would be helpful if you knew first what Jesus' life looked like. How did he "do life," treat people, interact with his Heavenly Father, pray, consider differently cultured or differently colored people, be humble, worship, eat? What is Jesus' story of hope? What is the "hope" we have, and why? If you're not in the Bible, if you're not reading those stories and digging into how we should live, it will be difficult to know why and how we should be and can be transformed.

As followers of Jesus, we know why we live differently than the world. Peter knew why he was different. I mean, he had denied he even knew Jesus, even used curse words while Jesus was looking at him the night of Jesus' arrest and subsequent execution. Peter knew what Jesus had done for him. He'd lived the story. We are different because we know how much Jesus has done for us. We know we don't deserve it, but he has given us new life anyway.

So, when the world figuratively slaps us around and we have joy anyway or self-control or do not repay meanness with meanness—when we don't follow the world's script—people in the world take notice because it's different, refreshing, something novel. Peter is telling us to be ready in those moments to tell the reason we act differently. And in order to tell the reason with confidence, you and I have to commit to knowing the story of God, so we can know the different and varied ways we can tell with a smile why we act like Jesus.

In August 2017, southern Texas experienced Hurricane Harvey. At this time, the area is still far from recovered, although the storm has long since dissipated. According to newscasts, this natural disaster could possibly have caused upward of $180 billion in damages.

In our country, we are currently seeing elevated racial tensions, police strains with the public, and demographic anxieties. But in such a difficult and broken moment in the aftermath of Harvey, people in south Texas have set aside the tensions and embraced helping one another, living out the story of Jesus. Anyone watching the story, including media outlets, are commenting on how people have stopped fighting about things that do not matter and are, well, looking like Jesus—extending compassion, praying together, and offering assistance without compensation.

See, unless you and I make a decision to make some time each day—time that is not distracted by social media, cell phones, and petty things that really don't matter—we will not be able to tap into the story of Jesus and be able to confidently tell others the reason for the hope we have in him and the life he's called us to live out. We will not know how we are to act, treat strangers, live healthily, be emotionally and mentally stable, handle money, raise our children, love our spouses, consider our neighbors, focus on things that matter, or respect authority figures. Aren't you tired of not having the peace in your life that only Jesus can offer? Aren't you ready to have different results in your life than you're experiencing right now?

If so, take some time, right now in the back of this book to think about the course of your daily schedule. If you're honest and earnest about knowing who the person is that Jesus has called you to be, when during the day or night will you take time to read Jesus' words? What fifteen minutes out of your twenty-four-hour day are you willing to set aside to better know how to be healthy for you and your relationships? What part of your day are you willing to dedicate to knowing the story of God intimately, so that you can give the reason, when asked, for the hope you have in Jesus the Christ, the Son of God, the Creator of all things, the Lover of you?

You have been saying you were going to do this. Tomorrow is right now. It's time to discover the beautiful blueprint for life that Jesus has for you. It's time to exchange that self-harming script the world has given you, and discover the happiness you can have with the person you were created to be. Come on, get going—don't wait. Get into Jesus' story and become part of his story. I promise, it's a page-turner.

Study Guide for Chapter Seven: Set

Read the text:

1 Peter 3:15–16:

You must worship Christ as Lord of your life. And if someone asks about your hope as a believer, always be ready to explain it. But do this in a gentle and respectful way. Keep your conscience clear. Then if people speak against you, they will be ashamed when they see what a good life you live because you belong to Christ.

Open:

Have you ever been a part of a sports team or work team? Explain. Were there any weird rules you had to abide by? What were they?

Dig in:

1. Peter is writing to first-century Christians who are being persecuted by the culture. They had never known what "church" means, like we do today. If you could reach back in time to encourage them, what would you say to them? How would you urge them in their spiritual journey?

2. Peter encouraged the church to worship Jesus as Lord and King. How difficult would this have been in the Roman culture where Caesar was god and king? What obstacles would they no doubt have encountered in their everyday lives?

3. When do you remember your very first "church" activity? What did you do? How did it impact you?

4. Read Romans 12:1–2. How do Paul's comments support and reinforce Peter's statement to worship Jesus as Lord?

5. Based upon Peter's statement, how important is it that each of us, as followers of a risen Savior, knows the gospel story? If we are honest, could we take someone who doesn't know Jesus and enthusiastically show them the reason we have hope?

6. Some would believe the above question is the church pastor's job. However, we are called a priesthood of believers (see 1 Peter 2:5–9), indicating that each of us has an equal task and are not relying on one person to do it all for us. How motivating and convicting is Peter's comment that each of us should be ready to share our story? What should change in your life, to facilitate a better knowledge of the story?

7. What can our church do differently to help all believers be prepared to give the reason for our hope in Jesus Christ? List them.

CHAPTER EIGHT

ILLOGICAL:
FOLLOW EVEN WHEN IT DOESN'T
MAKE SENSE

*B*rian Regan is my absolute favorite comedian. If you've never heard of him, I'm begging you, find him on youtube.com and begin actually losing weight because you're laughing so much. I believe speakers—or in this case, comedians—can really, truly connect with people from their generation.

Brian and I connect. Well, he doesn't know me from Adam, but I connect with his stories because I have lived them. It's almost as if we ran in the same crowd and got into the same trouble as we grew up. He simply has a knack of taking me back to my childhood and reliving memories that are funny now, although in the moment they happened they were very stressful.

For instance, Brian talks about coming home from school and being told to go outside and play. He and his brothers would make up games to play. One of those games was fun but dangerous. It was definitely one of those games you would not tell your mom about unless you had to divulge exactly what you had been doing when the accident occurred.

The game Brian and his brothers would play was in the street. They would create elaborate ramps for their bicycles. The brothers would jump over things or see who could jump the greatest distance or who could spin their front tire and handlebars the most times before coming down. You know, fun stuff all boys like to do.

Brian mentions the first time they built a huge ramp to jump their bikes. Their brother started at the end of the street. He came barreling down the road and hit the ramp exactly as intended. However, that's as far as they had thought through the scenario. While his brother was up in the air for what felt like miles, he screamed in terror at his brothers on the ground, "What do I do now?" Neither Brian nor the other onlookers had any idea, so his brother hit the ground, wiped out, and broke his arm.

There are moments when you know and realize your mom is going to kill you if you are not already dead. Brian says that this was one of those moments. They were trying to fix his brother's arm yelling, "Get some leaves!" After realizing all their efforts were fruitless, someone was elected to go in and tell mom.

Brian was not going to be the one, so he sent his brother in, who slid into the house like Richard Petty finishing Daytona. But even in the hurriedness, his brother remained calm, knowing he didn't need to upset his mom. As calm as a gentle breeze across the wheat plains of Kansas, the brother asked their mom if she was going to the grocery store soon—and that, if she was going to the grocery store, she might want to take her son to the hospital. "I'm not sure my brother's arm should bend the way it's currently bending" was the calm statement from a guy who knew his brother needed a different type of experience that included x-rays and a cast. As said earlier, Brian and I could have been friends—close middle school friends.

When I was in the seventh grade, we lived in a little town called Glenwood which was located about thirty miles from Hot Springs, Arkansas. I grew up in a preacher's home. We were raised with love and affection, but there were rules. One of those rules involved the school week and dinnertime.

I have two younger brothers. Part of our weekly process was going to school and coming home like most American kids in the early 1980s. We were told that when we came home from school, we had to take off our school clothes and put on our play clothes to go outside and play—and play clothes were simply school clothes that were now too tight! Mom would call us in for dinner but until then, we had to discover how to entertain ourselves until the dinner bell rang.

In Glenwood, we lived in the church parsonage; it was a ranch-style house, meaning it was one level. The church owned the house, so we didn't have a lot of say over what we could do to it. There was a separate garage in the backyard where we kept several things in storage, including our ladder.

On this particular day, I was looking for an experience— you know, something to excite me, something to "break the rules" of safety and adventure. For this seventh grader desiring to expand his resume of "conquered mountains," I wanted to be a little dangerous but not too dangerous. I wanted to feel life. I had longed for the courage to feel the wind in my hair and master something I had thought about but never accomplished. Today was going to be that day.

So, once I put on my too-tight play clothes, I walked out to the garage in our back yard to retrieve our ladder. I took that ladder and leaned it up against our house, on the end farthest away from the kitchen where my mom was making dinner. I didn't want to worry her. And once I had secured that ladder, I walked intently, purposefully, determined to achieve my goal. I walked to the side of the house where I had parked my banana-seat bicycle. Oh, you now see where I'm going, don't you? You've been there before. It's almost like a dare from a best friend. You can't lose face. You must follow through or people will not respect you, believe in you, or trust you anymore with what you say you're going to do.

With the determination of Evel Knievel jumping Snake River in 1974, I slowly walked my bike to the ladder. One rung at a time, my tiny seventy-pound body hoisted that bike up the ladder until I reached the roofline. With a great deal of grunting and sweat, I climbed onto the roof and pulled my bike up there with me. Once I stood up and looked at the ground below, I thought to myself that this might not have been such a good idea. However, I was committed now. There was no backing out.

Being on the roof with my bike was a mixture of fear and adrenaline. The crowd noise inside you is so loud. One voice in your head saying, "You are the bomb," while the other voice says, "You are a complete idiot." It was the kind of rush one gets on the Powder Keg roller coaster at Silver Dollar City near Branson, Missouri. You are strapped in and there's no getting out of that seat. You know in 3-2-1, that car you are in is going to fly from zero to sixty in just three seconds.

With the adrenaline pumping, I walked my bike to the crest of the roof where I surveyed all of creation—on my street. No one was watching. No one knew what was about to go down. No one knew my plan for success. As deeply as a seventh-grader can think, I had surmised the layout of the roof, the PSI in the bike tires, the wind direction, approximate speed needed to reach before launch, and of course the most important thing in the whole formula (if this was going to work): the gutter.

You see, I had determined that if timed correctly, the gutter on the house would be the last *level* area my bike tire would touch, giving me the opportunity to pop a wheelie. With the perfectly performed wheelie in place, I would land on the ground flawlessly parallel to the ground, which was ten feet below my launch point. Impeccable plan, right?

The time had come for launch. Mom would call us for dinner soon. It was now or never. I would be a man of my word. I would accomplish today what I had refused to do so many other days. It was going to be epic! Have you ever said that phrase but the second you began your journey, you knew it was never a good idea?

Taking one huge gulp of air, I began my quick journey down the roof, watching the gutter the entire time. Thankfully, it never moved. However, I don't know if you have ever realized this one little important piece of information that's not highly discussed among seventh-grade boys: Gutters are not created, not built, to hold any weight. That's not their purpose. They're created to divert water during rainy weather to a downspout and then safely away from the house.

Well, the second my bike tire came in contact with that gutter, it simply folded away toward the soffit of the house. Without any support to pop my perfect wheelie, allowing me a safe landing ten feet below, I began my very fast journey downward toward the bushes just outside one of the windows of the house.

The ride down lasted no more than two seconds. Can I say I have never been more excited to have a box hedge around the front of our house? God does work in mysterious ways. I still thank God to this day for the person who planted that row of lush greenness! If memory serves me correctly, I ran inside to the kitchen and hugged my mom like maybe never before. Parents, a heads-up: When your child comes out of nowhere and gives you a squeezing hug without you asking for it and tells you he or she loves you, you know that kid almost killed him or herself, unintentionally.

You have to admit, while ill-advised, that was one brave thing to do. I mean, the guts it took to follow through with what you said you would do. Making good on a promise you had made. One can talk all day long but unless you actually do something, the story is still unfinished.

Once there was this friend group in the Bible who had made gutsy promises. You may have never heard their names before now. But they were incredibly brave men who knew they had a story to tell. Their names were (originally) Hananiah, Mishael, and Azariah. Each one was a man of God, a member of the tribe of Judah, but they were exiles in Babylon under King Nebuchadnezzar. Their names meant "God is Gracious," "Who is like God?," and "God is helped," respectively.

One thing I love about the ancient world is that names had real meaning. Each one of these men who loved God and worshipped the one and only God found themselves in a moment of their history to be brave in a culture that didn't know or appreciate the God of Israel. Sound familiar to our current culture in America?

It's tough to make good on promises you made, especially when no one else has agreed to support you. These three men of God found themselves in a distant land, surrounded by powerful people who read from a different script.

Maybe you find yourself in a similar situation. Maybe your distant land is a workplace that bullies you because you choose to be kind and gracious and turn the other cheek. Maybe your unfamiliar territory is your neighborhood, surrounded by families that have a different opinion of how to raise a family. Maybe you must dwell in the middle of a family who puts other things above what you feel God has called on you to do, and you endure the looks that ostracize you from being fully accepted.

You see, King Nebuchadnezzar thought a great deal of himself. Babylon was located in the general area of current-day Iran and Iraq. Nebuchadnezzar was the world power. He did not rule a democracy. He was a monarch. It was his decision alone when any decision was made—for much of the known world! He liked the idea of controlling the people, even their worship. When you have an ego like his, you just meddle in everything to get people to do what you believe is so wise.

So Nebuchadnezzar commissioned a golden statue created for his people, including his conquered people, to bow down and worship. The text tells us it was huge. Imagine a nine-story building. It was that tall and that wide, and made out of gold. You would be able to see it for miles, rising out of the ground like the Dallas Cowboys' AT&T Stadium where "America's Team" plays.

On opening day, the first day of worship, all the king's officials stood by the idol made of gold. The herald announced that at the playing of the king's orchestra, everyone was to bow down to the golden ninety-foot idol. There would be no exceptions. Not one person could say, "No, not today, I'm busy." And so, the orchestra played on opening day and every knee bowed toward the golden idol.

Can you imagine that type of power today? With the sound of music (not the movie), everyone, no matter their age, race, skin color, how cool you thought you were, everyone would stop what they were doing to bow down to this new golden image. Everyone stopped what they were doing and took a knee—except three guys in the king's court who had made a promise to their God, the God of Israel, the real and only God in all the world.

Think for a moment. Every. Single. Person. Everyone in your school or your workplace or your neighborhood or your local fun park or your family goes down on a knee except you. You are the only one left standing, which brings immediate attention to you. The spotlight is on you and why you are not conforming. It takes bravery to be a nonconformist. Paul reminds us of this in his epic theological letter to the church in Rome:

> Don't copy the behavior and customs of this world, but let God transform you into a new person by changing the way you think. Then you will learn to know God's will for you, which is good and pleasing and perfect (Romans 12:2).

These men from Judah, men who honored God with their actions as well as their lips, made a decision to be brave on this day even if the spotlight were on them. I guess I should tell you why I think they are so brave: Not only would they be the only ones standing, the king had also decreed that anyone who didn't bow down would be burned alive!

Now, I know you have been burned. Maybe it was the curling iron or the clothes iron that brushed your skin. Maybe you got too close to the campfire one night while roasting marshmallows for s'mores. You and I have felt heat before, but not on the level promised by the king. Can you imagine that pain you felt for a while after touching something hot for only one second? And now the promise is that you'll be thrown into a furnace big enough for several people if you do not bow down. Folks, this is where the rubber meets the road. Would you be able to withstand the pressure? Could you stand for what is right, knowing what the consequence will be? Your life . . . ended.

The example these three men show us is incredible, extreme, and absolutely devoted. They love and fear God, the God of Israel. They have already made the plan to serve only God, the God of Israel. They have prayed and fasted, knowing the day would come when they would have to be brave and make a choice to follow God, the God of Israel. Their adrenaline is pumping. They are on the peak of their roof, looking at the guttering. The time has come to show their true colors. The world's orchestra begins to play. The whole world touches the ground. They stand to hold hands with God, the God of Israel.

The king sees their defiance and approaches. The three will not cave in to being bullied to do something different than what God desires of them. The text says the king is so angry his face actually becomes distorted. I imagine something like Captain Kirk's face in the movie *Star Trek II: The Wrath of Khan*, realizing he's been left in the middle of a planet to be "buried alive" and screaming, "Khaaaannnnnn!"

Nebuchadnezzar's face changes shape . . . and color. The king is beside himself with rage. He is so furious. Someone would not concede to his wishes? Impossible. After all, he is the world power. How dare anyone not believe he is the biggest, richest, wisest, most powerful demigod on the planet? He is so fuming mad that he has his special human furnace heated to seven times the heat that already is boiling inside of it.

In one swoop, Nebuchadnezzar immediately has the three men of God from Judah arrested, bound, and thrown into the furnace that's hotter than a backyard grill on the Fourth of July in Arizona. In fact, it's so hot that the king's men who have been ordered to throw these defiant vagabonds into the hotter-than-hell furnace are liquefied (you heard me correctly) as they toss the insolent second-class citizens into the magma den.

The demigod king has a front-row seat to watch the unbelievable anguish of anyone who has the audacity, the unmitigated gall of disobeying his command. He can watch as their flesh curls away, exposing wet bone. He'll witness the torment on the faces of those who dare mock his authority and supreme power. King Nebuchadnezzar will see their very names obliterated from the face of the earth. It will be as if they never existed.

But as the king peers into the incinerator from a distance, he counts not three but four men in the blazing fire. He calls for a head count. "Weren't there only three men tossed into the fire?" It's confirmed. Only three protesters—three misfits—only three blokes. But the king has indeed counted four men. The king goes as far as to say the fourth is brightly lit and looks like a god.

Think about that statement for a moment. All four are walking around in this firebox. It's seven times the normal heat. How gloriously magnificent must be the angels who are at the Lord's command and fight for us! Even in the middle of this blaze, God's angel is shining so brightly that he stands out against the fire. The king realizes that these three men serve a god who is far greater than any he has ever known. Three men stand against a nation, and now the nation will kneel for other reasons.

The king calls out to the names you recognize from Sunday school, "Shadrach, Meshach, and Abednego, servants of the Most High God, come out! Come here!" (Dan. 3:26). The story tells us that when they stepped out of the furnace, not one stitch of their clothing was scorched, not one hair was singed; they didn't even smell like smoke! In one incredible moment, an entire nation and a king was brought to their knees in the revelation of the one true God of all gods and Lord of all lords. The king of Babylon, the empire that ruled the world, said, "There is *no other God!*"

So, what golden statue is the world putting in front of you? Where do you discover the pressure to conform to society around you? What boss or spouse or kid or best friend or coworker or neighbor is telling you to do something different from the way God has called you to live? How well do you know your heart? What is your answer going to be when culture asks you to take a knee? Do you have the resolve these three men of God had?

It's difficult to do this journey all alone. Do you have two others who are walking with you who have the same spiritual goals as you? Others who will stand with you to push back the world's agenda and reveal the beautiful interference of God?

My prayer is you know deeply and intimately the God who loves you—who gave his Son for you so that you might live and prosper. May you feel God's mighty right arm lift you up. May you know the certainty you can have because God will never leave you. May you have the courage to stand when others take their knees. May you be empowered to voice God's hope and say like our three Judean believers, "The God whom we serve is able to save us. He will rescue us . . . but even if he doesn't, we will never serve another god."

Study Guide for Chapter Eight: Illogical

Read the text:

Daniel 3:

King Nebuchadnezzar made a gold statue ninety feet tall and nine feet wide and set it up on the plain of Dura in the province of Babylon. Then he sent messages to the high officers, officials, governors, advisers, treasurers, judges, magistrates, and all the provincial officials to come to the dedication of the statue he had set up. So all these officials came and stood before the statue King Nebuchadnezzar had set up.

Then a herald shouted out, "People of all races and nations and languages, listen to the king's command! When you hear the sound of the horn, flute, zither, lyre, harp, pipes, and other musical instruments, bow to the ground to worship King Nebuchadnezzar's gold statue. Anyone who refuses to obey will immediately be thrown into a blazing furnace."

So at the sound of the musical instruments, all the people, whatever their race or nation or language, bowed to the ground and worshiped the gold statue that King Nebuchadnezzar had set up.

But some of the astrologers went to the king and informed on the Jews. They said to King Nebuchadnezzar, "Long live the king! You issued a decree requiring all the people to bow down and worship the gold statue when they hear the sound of the horn, flute, zither, lyre, harp, pipes, and other musical instruments. That decree also states that those who refuse to obey must be thrown into a blazing furnace. But there are some Jews—Shadrach, Meshach, and Abednego—whom you have put in charge of the province of Babylon. They pay no attention to you, Your Majesty. They refuse to serve your gods and do not worship the gold statue you have set up."

Then Nebuchadnezzar flew into a rage and ordered that Shadrach, Meshach, and Abednego be brought before him. When they were brought in, Nebuchadnezzar said to them, "Is it true, Shadrach, Meshach, and Abednego, that you refuse to serve my gods or to worship the gold statue I have set up? I will give you one more chance to bow down and worship the statue I have made when you hear the sound of the musical instruments. But if you refuse, you will be thrown immediately into the blazing furnace. And then what god will be able to rescue you from my power?"

Shadrach, Meshach, and Abednego replied, "O Nebuchadnezzar, we do not need to defend ourselves before you. If we are thrown into the blazing furnace, the God whom we serve is able to save us. He will rescue us from your power, Your Majesty. But even if he doesn't, we want to make it clear to you, Your Majesty, that we will never serve your gods or worship the gold statue you have set up."

Nebuchadnezzar was so furious with Shadrach, Meshach, and Abednego that his face became distorted with rage. He commanded that the furnace be heated seven times hotter than usual. Then he ordered some of the strongest men of his army to bind Shadrach, Meshach, and Abednego and throw them into the blazing furnace. So they tied them up and threw them into the furnace, fully dressed in their pants, turbans, robes, and other garments. And because the king, in his anger, had demanded such a hot fire in the furnace, the flames killed the soldiers as they threw the three men in. So Shadrach, Meshach, and Abednego, securely tied, fell into the roaring flames.

But suddenly, Nebuchadnezzar jumped up in amazement and exclaimed to his advisers, "Didn't we tie up three men and throw them into the furnace?"

"Yes, Your Majesty, we certainly did," they replied.

"Look!" Nebuchadnezzar shouted. "I see four men, unbound, walking around in the fire unharmed! And the fourth looks like a god!"

Then Nebuchadnezzar came as close as he could to the door of the flaming furnace and shouted: "Shadrach, Meshach, and Abednego, servants of the Most High God, come out! Come here!"

So Shadrach, Meshach, and Abednego stepped out of the fire. Then the high officers, officials, governors, and advisers crowded around them and saw that the fire had not touched them. Not a hair on their heads was singed, and their clothing was not scorched. They didn't even smell of smoke!

Then Nebuchadnezzar said, "Praise to the God of Shadrach, Meshach, and Abednego! He sent his angel to rescue his servants who trusted in him. They defied the king's command and were willing to die rather than serve or worship any god except their own God. Therefore, I make this decree: If any people, whatever their race or nation or language, speak a word against the God of Shadrach, Meshach, and Abednego, they will be torn limb from limb, and their houses will be turned into heaps of rubble. There is no other god who can rescue like this!"

Then the king promoted Shadrach, Meshach, and Abednego to even higher positions in the province of Babylon.

Open:

Have you ever been bullied? Describe the situation and how you overcame it.

Dig in:

1. These three guys were captives in a foreign land. Babylon did not create margin to worship any god but their own. What obstacles would these three men have to overcome, in general? What was their world like?

2. Nebuchadnezzar was the king. He was the ruling authority. What he said would need to be done. Yet these men made a decision to defy that authority. Our current country seems to be in constant strain with the law of the land and the civil authorities. When is it okay to push back against authority?

3. Read Romans 13:1–7. How does Paul remind us as followers of Jesus to live under our current authorities? How is that difficult? How does that come easy for you?

4. Nebuchadnezzar creates a physical idol to worship. Although we don't really see "idols" in our country, metaphoric idols exist. What are some of those idols we must create boundaries against today? List those things that are in conflict with us truly worshiping God.

5. What needs to happen in your life, for you to feel confident enough to stand up to the bullying that might occur in your spiritual walk? How do you become strong to live out your life for God's glory? How can you encourage others to stand for the hope we have in Jesus?

6. What are some things this church can do to help you stand against the "idols" of our culture? How can this church cultivate a spirit of "God is the most important thing" in our lives?

CHAPTER NINE

REAL:
PLAYING HIDE AND SEEK

J grew up a WASP male in the good ol' US of A. That acronym stands for white, Anglo-Saxon, Protestant— you don't have to live in America to grow up that way, but I did. When you grow up, you're typically in a bubble whether you realize it or not. It's not true for every family but most families tend to encircle their clan with other people who look like them. It tends to be less messy, more comfortable, less need to "keep an eye on" what other people are doing—or so we tell ourselves. Generally speaking, while living in America the folks who hung around us were a lot like us in our cultural expectations, where we went to church, our skin color, where our schools were located, where we shopped for groceries, and of course the neighborhood where we found our house.

I was blessed in that my father was not only a preacher but also a missionary. I had the pleasure of living two years in Cameroon, West Africa, and a year on those South Pacific islands called Vanuatu. Vanuatu is located beside the Fiji Islands. In 2004, CBS aired the ninth season of the TV show *Survivor* from Efate, Vanuatu. That's the town where I used to live! Small world isn't it?

We moved back to the US in 1980 and set up housekeeping in the state of Arkansas. I lived in Arkansas from the seventh grade through my early twenties. Like most, I surrounded myself with people who looked like me, acted like me, ate similar food as me. It was not hard interacting with people like me. But eventually, I graduated high school and struck out on my own as I headed to college in another Arkansan town.

Leaving home was the best thing for me. I say the best because it started me down a path of asking some real questions of myself for the first time in my life. I mean I was able to experience life outside "the bubble."

My eyes were opened to a brand-new world. I was hanging with folks who went clubbing every weekend. I had never experienced music so loud, lights so dim, and an ever-present smell of cheap cologne. These folks went home early in the morning and didn't really care about whom they woke up beside the next morning. It was excitingly fun, and an adrenaline rush every weekend. Looking back, I find it interesting how our enemy creates those feelings when we turn away from the path God has created for us to live.

Those first five years of my young adult life were spent wandering, experiencing life with Tim's agenda, exploring strange new worlds where I saw things I had never experienced when I lived in "the bubble." While initially euphoric, the truth is that week in and week out, this lifestyle can tire you, break you, make you spend money you don't have, physically harm you, and without a doubt spiritually wreck your life until you finally wake up one morning believing, "This can't be all there is in life." There must be something more than this wasteful, selfish, shallow existence. There must be a better, healthier plan than all of this.

In the mid-'60s, Robert Kennedy was campaigning for the Democratic nomination for the president of the United States. He undertook a five-day crisscrossing, meet-and-greet in Harlem in New York City. Robert had a guide who took him on that five-day journey. Kennedy took time to talk to those who were out of work. He shook hands with those who were working hard for small wages, to put food on the table for their families. He walked past boarded-up houses and trash-strewn streets. He talked to citizens outside of burned-out buildings. He watched as shopkeepers eked out a meager living to make their lives just a little better.

The guide who was with him asked, "Why do you come here so often, Mr. Kennedy?" To which Robert replied, "I found something out about myself. I don't live in the real world. My world is not the real world."

I too realized the world in which I was choosing to live was not the real world. I knew in my heart there was a God who loved me, who might even forgive me if the stories were true. I knew that someone wrapped up in himself creates a very small package. Deep down, I knew that the world I was living in was not the real one. I wanted to be part of the real world—the one God had chosen for me, created for me, the one where he wanted to use me in his story. So, leaving behind everything that had become comfortable to me, I began looking for crevices of light where I could quietly join God in the story he was playing out in the world. I began to move out of my dark bubble albeit ever so slowly, becoming vulnerable to the story that included everyone in God's creation, all those who are aware and unaware of his calling.

Over time and the last twenty-five years, I have done a lot of traveling around the world for the cause of Christ. I count it such a privilege to be an active part of God's story, knowing the whole time who I used to be—and knowing the whole time that God has forgiven me and is thrilled that I have chosen him and his ways over all things in my life.

I have grown and traveled and discovered beautiful people I never knew existed. Gypsies in Croatia, the Taino in Jamaica, the French who speak so beautifully, the Cameroons rich with tribal culture, the Vanuatuans who sing with Moana how the ocean calls them, the Aussies who always throw another shrimp on the barbie just for you, and yes, even Minnesotans who graciously accepted two young southerners into their clan for a very short while.

You see, leaving home was good for me. It made me wrestle with what I believed. Leaving home made me grapple with why I believed it *that way*. It made me positively consider other people who didn't look like me or act like me or eat like me or believe in "church" the way I had been taught. It made me think about cultural biases. It made me reflect on sexual preferences and differences. It made me consider my theology and philosophy, compared to what Jesus said actually really mattered. Did I think like Jesus? Was I open to being uncomfortable like Jesus says I will probably be if I follow him? How was I prepared to get along with other people who did not look like me? Based upon Jesus' teachings, was I living in the real world or my world?

Paul, in his letter to the church in Rome, about 57 AD, said it this way, quoting directly from the lips of Jesus the Christ:

Owe nothing to anyone—except for our obligation to
love one another. If you love your neighbor, you will

fulfill the requirements of God's law. For the commandments say, "You must not commit adultery. . . .
murder. . . . steal. . . . covet." These—and other such
commandments—are summed up in this one com-
mandment: "Love your neighbor as yourself." Love
does no wrong to others, so love fulfills the requirements of God's law (Rom. 13:8–10).

What I know is that it's easier to love and show that love
when I have everything in common with those around me.
When I'm in "the bubble," it's easy to do what Jesus calls us to
do. But what happens when I pop the bubble and realize Jesus
is talking about his entire creation, not just the assembly line of
look-alikes? What happens when I am so wrapped up in myself
that I can't see past the weekend? What happens when I don't
give my story over to the greatest storyteller ever?

You may have witnessed the horrific demonstration in
August 2017 in Charlottesville, Virginia. White nationalists
gathered to let the world know their "bubble" was better than
anyone else's. More inclusive counter-protesters gathered to be
a voice for those outside the white nationalist bubble. Violence
erupted and at the end of the interaction Heather Heyer, who
was a counter-protester; Lt. Jay Cullen; and Trooper Berke Bates
were dead. In total, thirty-four people were injured—all because
someone thought their bubble was better than the next person's. Unfortunately, people in our world wake up every morning just to hate, bully, and belittle. They live like that because
they are insecure in themselves and know little about how Jesus
has called us to live.

You see, Jesus put no qualifiers on his statements in Mark
12. He simply said, "Love God. Love people." He called us to

love people. Love people with a different skin color. Love people with a different religious creed. Love people with a sexual preference that differs from yours. Love people who hail from a different part of the world than you. Love people who live in a different tax bracket than you do. Love people who vote differently than you (seriously?). Yep. Love people who don't cheer for the Dallas Cowboys. Love people who get their mail in a different zip code than you. Love people who have no education, and those who have more education than you. Love people who wear turbans. Love people who have a prayer mat. Just simply love all people.

Jesus says that the love he offers is for everyone. Paul says in Romans 1:16 (emphasis added), "I am not ashamed of this Good News about Christ. It is the power of God at work, saving *everyone* who believes."

Think about what Peter said, the disciple handpicked by Jesus himself and who led the church in Jerusalem. In his great sermon on the day of Pentecost, Peter told everyone that Jesus was for, well, everyone. Toward the end of the sermon, Peter reminded all those who were listening, "This promise [of salvation] is to you, to your children, and to those far away— *all* who have been called by the Lord our God" (Acts 2:39, emphasis added)

As one reads through the letters of Paul, it is undeniable that Paul is hoping to get all his readers, then and now, to see that God's bubble is huge. God doesn't want to lose anyone. God wants his entire creation in relationship with him. Paul wants all of us, as followers of Jesus, to see what it looks like when we choose to pop our bubbles and enter into the inclusive story God is creating in the world.

You can almost feel the emotional urgency Paul uses as he writes these words for us to live by in his letter to the Romans:

Don't just pretend to love others. Really love them. Hate what is wrong. Hold tightly to what is good. Love each other with genuine affection, and take delight in honoring each other. Never be lazy, but work hard and serve the Lord enthusiastically. Rejoice in our confident hope. Be patient in trouble, and keep on praying. When God's people are in need, be ready to help them. Always be eager to practice hospitality.

Bless those who persecute you. Don't curse them; pray that God will bless them. Be happy with those who are happy, and weep with those who weep. Live in harmony with each other. Don't be too proud to enjoy the company of ordinary people. And don't think you know it all!

Never pay back evil with more evil. Do things in such a way that everyone can see you are honorable. Do all that you can to live in peace with everyone (Rom. 12:9–17).

I remember on my way back to God, Robin and I found a small church with whom to connect in the town of Owatanna, Minnesota. Robin and I loved working with them. They knew nothing about our personal worldly history. We had a new love for God and a desire to join in Kingdom work. Randy, the preacher, asked us to jump in and help with teaching kid's classes and leading singing. We were so excited to be included! On Sunday nights, we were part of Randy's small group that met at his house to study the Bible more in depth. Several people from church, and locals with whom Randy was studying, would attend.

I remember one guy, we'll call him Travis, was coming out of a very dark place. He had been studying with Randy and wanted to turn his life around, but it was a real challenge. Travis had been involved in animal sacrifice and satanic worship. He had been part of a gang. The gang, it was said, had actually murdered someone. He had been part of a "bubble" that I knew absolutely nothing about. As we listened to his story week after week, he seemed to me to be someone God would not be too interested in helping. He had been far away and I wasn't too sure he could be saved.

Now that I'm a little more mature in my faith, I'm embarrassed about my thoughts back then. We *all* need God's salvation. We *all* have fallen short of God's expectation. We *all* were far away. We *all*, no matter how deep or light we believe our sin, need Jesus the Christ.

I find it interesting, as we consider moral failure in other people, that we never look at our own lives very closely. We can see failings in others but if we don't extend *love* to people, we don't count that as failure. I mean, I could live in my neighborhood week after week, year after year, and have zero interaction with my neighbors—never reach out and offer a home cooked meal in the event of a death, offer to mow the yard when a neighbor is out of work, or watch the kids when someone is sick. We may never reach out to help those who have been affected by natural disasters or impacted by refugee migration. I mean, nothing would be said negatively of me; it's not a scandal. Why?

Because for some reason we aren't haunted by a lack of love. We are "okay" with living in our bubble and never stepping outside.

Jesus talks about living in our own bubble, peering through our own haze to look at other people. In the Sermon on the Mount in the Gospel of Matthew, Jesus says that we often point out the smallest speck of wood, a splinter, in our neighbor's eye when in fact there is a huge piece of railway lumber in our own eye. Jesus is calling us to stop our unloving lifestyle and pour love into those around us who have made different choices than we have made, those with tattoos and piercings, an addictive habit, who are same-sex attracted—in other words, those who look and act unlike than we do. He's calling us to imitate him in every way, even when we feel stretched, uncomfortable, squeamish.

See, Jesus is calling us to use that wooden beam in our own eye to build bridges to those around us, not walls. But too often, we're more interested in protecting the bubble we live in, so we build those walls.

A great example of building walls, once again, is the disciple Peter. Now remember, he was hand-picked by Jesus. He preached boldly on the day of Pentecost on the steps of the Jerusalem temple, and the story tells us that three thousand men were baptized that day. That number doesn't include the women and children who were also baptized that day, so we know more than three thousand became believers that day. Peter was present, an arm's length away from Jesus, at the end of the Gospel of Matthew when Jesus reminded his followers to go out into the *whole world* and tell the story of Jesus . . . to *everyone!*

But Peter could also be a self-righteous, pride-filled man. He was prejudiced against anyone who was not part of his ethnic heritage, his way of life, his theology, his tribe. He was a

Jewish man. He would have been taught from a very young age that if you ever even brush up against a non-Jewish person, go home and wash off the contamination. He would have been instructed to never help a non-Jewish woman in childbirth in any way. That's just another non-Jew being brought into the world, and why would you want that to happen? Don't ever enter a Gentile's house (anyone who was not a Jew), and don't allow a Gentile into your own house because that would defile you, your family, and your home. These types of teachings would have been comfortable with Peter. It's what he had heard his entire life. But God needed to take Peter out of his comfort zone, out of his bubble, to let him see more clearly what Jesus' words and life were all about.

So in Acts 10, Peter has a vision to go see a man named Cornelius. Guess what? He's a Gentile. Oh, and he's also an officer in the Roman army—you know, the Roman army that has conquered the Jews and is a present force in Judea? Yet Peter is hearing God call him to a Roman, Gentile house. Talk about uncomfortable. Talk about out of the bubble. Peter's mind must have been racing. What if my tennis partner hears about this? What if my mom and dad know that I'm going to hang with someone they always told me to stay away from? What if the guys at church get wind that I went intentionally to see this guy and knew I would be defiled? Will they still be my friends? What if I did the very thing that I've been taught my whole life not to do?

As followers of Jesus, we don't live in fear of what others say. We lean into what God is saying.

God wins the day. Peter acquiesces to God's call to inclusive behavior although it's different, awkward, uncomfortable, and prickly. Peter says to Cornelius, after much interaction and discussion, "I see very clearly that God shows *no favoritism*. In every nation he accepts those who fear him and do what is right" (Acts 10:35, emphasis added).

Peter has begun to realize God's plan. God is going to include *everyone* in the offer of salvation. *Everyone* can be adopted into the family of God, regardless of their heritage. God treats *everyone* the same, although we create our own walls instead of bridges with the huge, burdensome pieces of wood in our eyes.

Small-bubble people create boundaries and walls when they compare black versus white.

Catholic versus Protestant.

Latino versus African-American.

Political liberal versus political conservative.

King James Version versus every other version.

Tattoos and piercing versus clean canvas.

American versus North Korean.

Straight versus same-sex attracted.

Graying senior versus Millennial.

Muslim versus Christian.

Rich versus poor.

'80s music lovers versus rap.

Educated versus uneducated.

Homeowner versus homeless.

What you and I need to realize is that "value" is what someone is willing to pay for something. The disciple named John, who wrote several books of the New Testament, reminds the persecuted churches in Asia Minor (modern-day Turkey) and us of our value to God:

> We know what real love is because Jesus gave up his life for us. So we ought to give up our lives for [others]. . . . God showed how much he loved us by sending his one and only Son into the world so that we might have eternal life through him. This is real love—not that we loved God, but that he loved us and sent [Jesus] as a sacrifice (1 John 3:16; 4:9–10).

You see, God has paid *the* highest price for you in his Son Jesus! He values you and all his creation. Salvation is for everyone! God said, "I'll take that wooden piece of railway lumber out of your eye and allow my son to die on it. By his wounds you will be healed; his punishment will bring you peace; he will be pierced for your offenses; he will be crushed in order to build a bridge for everyone."

The truth is, Jesus' love is for those who have been rape victims. His love is also for the rapists. His love is for frat boys and sorority girls. He loves the unchurched and those who have attended church since birth. He loves Hell's Angels and those who drive a Prius. Jesus loves those who have been physically and emotionally abused. He loves the abuser as well. Jesus loves the kids who have two moms or two dads. He loves those who find themselves addicted to heroin, alcohol, or pornography. Jesus loves those who are clean and sober. Jesus loves single moms and single dads. He loves those who keep giving in to temptation. And Jesus loves you!

You see, a gospel that isn't for everyone, everywhere is not a gospel for anyone, anywhere. God's dream for his church is that it would be an *everyone* kind of place. His church is called to be a hospital for his creation, not a castle to hide behind nor a club with an exclusive clientele. God's hope is that we would start being his ambassadors, building bridges to the broken, messy places in our world to imitate and look like Jesus.

As we make a decision to step outside our bubble and into the world to which God has called us, it does not mean we compromise truth. We simply speak the gospel message in love with lovely actions. Too many times we, like Peter, segregate ourselves to "stay clean." Sometimes listening to the quiet whispers in our own minds, we are converted to believe, "If I love on people who don't look like me or act like me or believe like me, I am condoning their life, their actions, their words, their style of living." I am reminded time and time again that we are called to imitate Jesus in our loving, but not in our decisions on who gets salvation and who does not. That is Jesus' call to us: Love this messy world. Offer the one thing that this world does not offer. Offer hope and the story that goes with it.

Have you ever played hide and seek? You know, the game where one person counts to one hundred while covering their eyes and everyone else goes to find their special hiding place? Of course you have! It's an age-old game that none of us are ever too old to play. We've played it with our kids, grandkids, friends. . . . In truth, everyone playing wants to be found. That is part of the fun. You hide somewhere. You find a chair, a curtain, or a closet to hide behind. The adrenaline is pumping as you hear footsteps approach. Someone opens the closet door where you are located and everyone starts smiling and laughing. We all really want to be found.

However, there are people in your life—close friends, long-time coworkers, family members—who you would swear really do not want to be found. You feel it in their words, their actions, their emotions. They seem negative. They've been hurt and have given up. They don't want to be bothered. They are not interested in a conversation. But if you pay attention, if you are conscious while around them, if you listen closely to what they say, you will see a foot or a hand sticking out from behind wherever they are hiding. They are saying ever so cautiously that they want to be known—they want to be loved.

So, in the back of this book, take some time to be honest with yourself. Write down one area of your life, one person maybe, who makes you uncomfortable. Take some time to think about opportunity. Pray to God to give you wisdom and words. Allow Jesus to lead you through the uncomfortable moment, the prickly thought, the awkward conversation, or the sensitive idea. It's time to build those bridges and tear down those walls. It's time we stopped just calling ourselves followers of the Rabbi and allow our actions to indicate whom we really are trying to imitate. Go get 'em, tiger! I know that Jesus will be with you as you take that first step.

Study Guide for Chapter Nine: Real

Read the text:

Romans 12:9–18:

Don't just pretend to love others. Really love them. Hate what is wrong. Hold tightly to what is good. Love each other with genuine affection, and take delight in honoring each other. Never be lazy, but work hard and serve the Lord enthusiastically. Rejoice in our confident hope. Be patient in trouble, and keep on praying. When God's people are in need, be ready to help them. Always be eager to practice hospitality.

Bless those who persecute you. Don't curse them; pray that God will bless them. Be happy with those who are happy, and weep with those who weep. Live in harmony with each other. Don't be too proud to enjoy the company of ordinary people. And don't think you know it all!

Never pay back evil with more evil. Do things in such a way that everyone can see you are honorable. Do all that you can to live in peace with everyone.

Open:

Pretend for a moment that you're no longer here. Reflect on your life. How would you like to be remembered? Why? What's important about being remembered well? Does that legacy affect the generations in your family who will come later?

Dig in:

1. How do we react to right and wrong? Is there a correct way to react to either?

2. What do different levels of honoring one another look like? List some ways we could honor each other. Name some ways we should honor others, but don't do a good job of it.

3. The text calls us to be patient in trouble. Is this easy? What does patience look like as a God-lover? What are some ways you have discovered that help you be more patient?

4. We are called to help God's people when they are in need. This is followed by a call to be hospitable. How much is too much . . . or is there a limit? What are practical ways we can be hospitable? When we are in need, why are we reluctant to reach out for help? By failing to reach out, do we deny other followers the ability to do ministry?

5. Discuss praying for those who persecute you. How difficult is that, and why? What spiritual disciplines can we incorporate into our lives, to be more purposeful in fulfilling this call?

6. Paul calls followers of Jesus to "live in peace and harmony with each other." How realistic is this? Describe ways you have discovered to live at peace with those with whom you really don't see eye-to-eye.

7. How can this church help mentor a spirit of living in peace, harmony, and hospitality? What are ways these ideas can be championed by this church and its leadership?

LOVE WITH ALL YOUR PHYSICALITY (STRENGTH)

"For I can do anything through Christ who gives me strength."

~Philippians 4:13

"Great thoughts speak only to the thoughtful mind, but great actions speak to all mankind."

~Emily P. Bissell,
American social worker and activist

"Be faithful in small things because it is in them that your strength lies."

~Mother Teresa,
missionary to India

"But those who trust in the LORD will find new strength.
They will soar high on wings like eagles.
They will run and not grow weary.
They will walk and not faint."

~Isaiah 40:31

Mark 12:30

"Love the LORD your God with all your . . .
strength (physical)"

CHAPTER TEN

MUSCLE:
YOU ARE THE LIGHT

*J*couldn't have been more proud of myself. I wanted to play football in junior high and high school. There were just two problems when I entered the seventh grade. First, I might have weighed all of sixty pounds wringing wet. I was what I called "wiry." Second, I did not know anything about football. Not one thing.

I remember the first day of end-of-summer practice. I showed up on the junior high football field in Glenwood, Arkansas. We had just moved to that little town, for my dad to take the preaching job at the church. The first week of practice we were issued shorts, a school shirt, and a helmet. The helmet was so big that my head rattled around like a BB pellet in a tin can. That first week, we ran and ran and ran. I was so glad when the weekend came. But Monday was coming and unbeknownst to me, I needed to make a decision.

Monday came. The school day flew by and, after school was over, I found myself back out on the football field standing in a line. I had on my shorts, school shirt, and my helmet buckled on securely. Ron Hill was the head coach. He was shouting instructions to which I was oblivious. And then suddenly, someone in front of me turned and asked, "What position are you going out for?" I did not know a thing about any position. Well, anyone who hasn't a clue what they are doing knows what comes next. I asked him the same question in return, to which he replied, "I am going out for quarterback."

I thought, "Quarterback—that has a nice ring." So I replied with a smile that I was going to do the same thing. I thought how clever I was because all I would have to do now is follow this guy, stand with him, watch what he does, imitate his actions, and I'll have it made.

Can you say, absolute utterly foolish? Little did I know, everyone would be looking at the quarterback. This position handled the ball every . . . single . . . down! I would be in the spotlight, but had no idea what I was doing. Every coach, every player, and eventually every person in the stands would be watching my every movement. Not to mention all eleven players on the other team would be trying to tattoo my jersey number on every hash mark on the field. Do you remember that I weighed about sixty pounds? But I'm getting ahead of myself.

So I get in the quarterback line with my new friend. I begin to watch other guys in my line and what they're doing. They go up to the line and put their hands right up against another guy's rear end. They say some words out loud. I begin to sweat on top of the sweat I already have from running. I realize at this point, I have made a grave error—but now I can't move. I'm paralyzed. I couldn't go to a different line even if I wanted. I'm going to have to go through with the biggest mistake I have made. Everyone is going to watch me screw up.

I get to the head of the line. I'm watching the guy in front of me take his rep. He squats down and puts his hands where no guy's hands should ever go. He says some words that sound like "hut, hut." The ball is given to him, and he turns and gives the ball to another fellow who lined up behind the quarterback position. The coaches say, "Good job! Okay, Hall, you're up." Oh. My. Goodness. It is my turn.

To my disbelief, I remember to do everything like I should do. I squat, take the ball after I yell those words, and turn to give it to the guy behind me. Except there's a problem: The running back isn't there. There's no one to whom I can hand the ball.

In half a second, I panic and turn to my right instead of my left. To my surprise, that's the side the running back is on, so I'm able to safely give the ball to him and he runs through the line. The coach says, "Wow! This one (talking about me) is actually pretty fast. He turned the wrong way but got it to the running back anyway."

I genuinely appreciated the coach's encouragement, but that would be the only time I ever touched the ball as a quarterback hopeful. I eventually became an offensive lineman—a sixty-pound right guard, to be exact.

What that first year taught me was if I want to be successful at this sport, I would really have to eat well, run often, and lift weights. I had to get bigger if I was going to be any good at football. So that's what I did.

We moved three times while I was in junior high and high school. All three locations, I played football. I stuck to the plan. I practiced hard. I ate well. I ran and lifted weights. By the time I reached my senior year of high school, I weighed 140 pounds. Not only that, but I secured a starting defensive position as a cornerback. That year, I made All-District. At 140 pounds, I benched 210 pounds, power-clinged 200 pounds, squatted 360 pounds, and had the school record for pushups.

So what does all this football talk have to do with a spiritual walk? In Mark 12, we are called to love the Lord our God . . . with all our strength. There will be times when you'll need muscle to do what God has called you to do. There will be moments when you sign up for something that will require your arms and legs.

The half-brother of Jesus, James, tells us disciples that following actually calls us to *do something*. James reminds us that we are called to love our neighbors as ourselves. He goes on to state "you believe that there is one God. Good for you! Even the demons believe this. . . . Can't you see that faith without good deeds [muscle] is useless?" (James 2:19–20).

There is a physical aspect to walking with Jesus. As stated in the last chapter, those moments call us to get out of our comfort area, get out of the recliner, get off the couch, get out of the donut box, and actually put our money where our mouth is.

For instance, early in Jesus' physical ministry on earth, he asks people to journey with him—to follow him. Jesus is walking on the shore of the Sea of Galilee near Capernaum in Judea. There are several businesses being run up and down the beach, and he happens upon one that is a typical family-run fishing trade. Jesus sees two young guys, probably in their late teens, who are throwing a net into the water. This is how they bring the bacon (or the fish) home, so to speak. They are doing something, but then Jesus asks them to do something else: "'Come and follow me, I will show you how to fish for people!' And they left their nets at once and followed him" (Matt. 4:19–20).

The text says they physically did something. They stopped doing one thing and started doing something that involved them being risky, adventurous, and maybe even defiant. When you want to follow Jesus, you may have to put your muscles to work.

Even the information about the early church in the book of the Acts of the Apostles just oozes with this idea of people, following Jesus, actually doing something. Check it out: The first believers in Jesus all had each other's back. They did life together. It doesn't look like they were very worried about missing the Monday night football game or the sale going on at Abercrombie and Fitch or playing video games until the break of dawn. I will concede that these things did not exist when the early church was launched, but there were certainly cultural equivalents.

In Acts 2, we find out exactly what kind of muscle the early Jesus-followers had. We discover they ate together regularly. The luxury we experience today with restaurants and fast food did not exist in the life of the early church. Get this: They actually had each other over to their houses and cooked for each other while talking about life, family, and how to look more like Jesus.

Think about our lives today. We get exhausted just *thinking* about having people over. I need to vacuum, mop the floors, clean the bathrooms, plant some new flowers at the entrance, mow the yard, spray the backyard for insects, buy groceries, start cooking early, set the table. Whew! All this work and no one has even arrived yet.

Once our guests arrive, we feel the need to be jovial, communicative, entertaining, and inclusive of every guest. That's emotional energy that the workday may have sucked right out of us.

Once our guests have gone for the night, the cleanup begins, including washing the eating utensils, plates, cups, pots and pans rinsed off and put in the dishwasher. We still need to wipe down all countertops and the table. If you're lucky, you're in bed by eleven. Some of you dozed off just thinking through all of the logistics. We think through all this and resign ourselves to just not inviting each other over.

But being in each other's lives as followers of Jesus is what we're called to do. That is *one* of many ways we show love. My wife and I have a saying, "We really do not know you unless your feet have been under our table." It's our little saying that reminds us, it takes some muscle when you're called to follow Jesus.

That first-century church knew that they had to be in each other's lives if they were going to survive and journey well. They knew it would take work. They were willing to do whatever was necessary in order to follow faithfully and encourage each other on the journey. But again, hospitality was only one piece of how they used muscle.

These incredible examples of Jesus-followers also gave of their own personal material possessions. The text tells us they sold property and possessions and shared the money with those in need. No one needed anything because everyone was taking care of, well, everyone.

Can you imagine people you know, followers of Jesus, selling a car to pay for your medical bills, or selling a field in order to help you pay off some debt? That was what the first Jesus-followers wanted to do. They were absolutely different than their culture. People in the community where the church existed . . . noticed. It would have been like lighting a match in a pitch-dark room. It's what Jesus said in Matthew during the Sermon on the Mount, "You are the light of the world—like a city on a hilltop that cannot be hidden. . . . [L]et your good deeds shine out for all to see, so that everyone will praise your heavenly Father" (Matt. 5:14, 16).

That first group of disciples also made a point to be together. The text says they met together daily at the temple and in their homes. It would appear that whenever something was going on, everyone wanted to be a part of it. The church, the people who claimed to follow the Rabbi from Nazareth, didn't want to miss a thing.

I think that maybe we've forgotten that it takes some muscle to make the time to be together, to eat together, to do things together. It takes intentionality. It takes leadership. It takes some stick-to-itiveness. It takes a desire to want to be with other people. It's going to take practice and working out. It's going to take us getting out of our comfortable space and opening our lives up to other people. If we believe we are truly called to love the Lord with all our strength, we are going to have to rethink how to work our muscles.

Have you listened to a new music album, and heard the singer say something that made you think, "Did I just hear that correctly?" You stop the song and hit the arrow back to relisten to those lyrics. I think many of us need to do this in life. We've lived the same way for so long, we've become comfortable. It's just what we do. I don't really have to think because I'm on autopilot. I go to work. I earn my paycheck. I come home every evening by five-thirty. I turn on the news. I go to bed. Next day, rinse, repeat.

What if, as followers of Jesus Christ, we began looking at life and our purpose through Jesus' eyes? What if we hit the pause button and asked ourselves some really hard questions, to which we already know the piercing answers? What would happen if we admitted that we really don't use our muscle in following Jesus? What would happen if we took ourselves off cruise control and reimagined an intentional lifestyle that screams that we love Jesus and each other?

If we embrace the life Jesus calls us to live out, we may find that we have become more joyful, peace-loving, kind, gentle, full of goodness, and glass-half-full kind of people who are loving life and pouring into other people because of our purpose. And what's our purpose? Sharing the story of the most incredible and awesome God we have ever known!

See, our ultimate example of strength is the life of Jesus. He used his power to bring us back into a relationship with God. According to Paul in his letter to the Philippian church, Jesus left heavenly glory, his kingship, his crown, his throne, and came to earth to walk as a human being for some thirty-three years. He used his power to bring those into community who were lonely, stand up for those who could not stand on their own, grasp those who could not use their hands, create perspective for those who could not see, give voice to those who could not speak, be a hearing aid for those who could not hear, and give life back to those who were dead, physically and spiritually. Jesus touched lives. Jesus interacted with culture. Jesus loved people and his Father.

Eventually, Jesus used the love he had demonstrated in strength to endure the worst humility. He was wrongfully arrested. He was tried in a kangaroo court. He was unceremoniously hit in the face, spit on, and slapped. He was mercilessly beaten by a Roman guard with a cat-of-nine-tails within an inch of losing life. He was forced to carry his heavy, unfinished instrument of his execution, naked through the streets of Jerusalem. He was torturously forced to walk up a hill outside of the City of David where he laid down on the piece of wood, while Roman soldiers expertly hammered crucifixion spikes into his wrists and ankles.

You see, Jesus loved you with all his strength, until his strength left him on that cross where he died. His muscle was to carry your sins away from you so you could once again have a relationship with God. The psalmist says that as far as the east is from the west, Jesus' work on that hill has removed your sin from you (Ps. 103:12)! What excitement! What joy! What a heart-wrenching story! Can you feel the overwhelming love of the Savior? Can you feel the weight of Jesus' love for you? Jesus thought that I, as small as I am, was worth all this strength.

The work Jesus did for me calls me to follow him. His work calls me to lay down my metaphoric net and follow him. It is the very least I can do to embrace all he's done for me. His example shows me, compels me, to use my strength for his glory. His work calls me to love on people and share my life with them— to imitate those first-century disciples who loved together, ate together, lived life together, and journeyed together.

Maybe right now you're saying that you really don't have muscle. Maybe you're saying right now that you're not sure how to hit pause and rethink what following the Rabbi means. Maybe you're conflicted about how to start sharing life with others who also call themselves "followers." Maybe you feel there is something hindering you from using the strength you have for his glory. Did you know that Paul, the apostle, felt the same way?

Paul writes to the church that met in a house in Corinth, and tells them to be everything God has called them to be. To live life with purpose. But Paul reveals to those followers that he has something that hinders him. We don't know exactly what it was. Some speculate that this refers to Jewish persecution from his opponents; other scholars believe it could have been his own memory of his past when he persecuted early Christ-followers; others have stated it could have been a carnal temptation or depression; while others indicate he had poor eyesight due to some physical ailment. Whatever it was, Paul uses his example to encourage believers like you and me: "That's why I take pleasure in my weaknesses, and in the insults, hardships, persecutions, and troubles that I suffer for Christ. For when I am weak, then I am strong" (2 Cor. 12:10).

Our challenge is to love God with all our strength, and to love people the same way. We go into our story knowing there will be weak moments, moments we don't want to get out of bed, moments when another "running lap" is required of us, moments when we think our schedules are full. But we know we are designated to be different from the world around us. We are called to shine in the darkness. We are christened to be leaders, even though we may be tired.

I want to encourage you to push the pause button in your life. Consider how you are using your strength for the story of God. Reflect on how your walk looks. Does it resemble those first-century Christians? What would you do differently as you follow? Turn to the back of this book right now and answer that question. If you could change it, what in your life would you change in order to be that light, that strength, that muscle for the glory of God?

Study Guide for Chapter Ten: Muscle

Read the text:

Matthew 5:13–16:

"You are the salt of the earth. But what good is salt if it has lost its flavor? Can you make it salty again? It will be thrown out and trampled underfoot as worthless.

"You are the light of the world—like a city on a hilltop that cannot be hidden. No one lights a lamp and then puts it under a basket. Instead, a lamp is placed on a stand, where it gives light to everyone in the house. In the same way, let your good deeds shine out for all to see, so that everyone will praise your heavenly Father."

Open:

Can you remember the first time your mom or dad really praised you for something? Tell the story. How did that make you feel? How did it affect you moving forward in your story?

Dig in:

1. What comes to mind when you think of darkness in the world? What are some current cultural issues that look like darkness in the world to you?

2. Have you ever had a literal mountaintop experience— like a hike to a mountaintop in Colorado or a look out the observatory in the Empire State Building in New York City? At the bottom and looking up at your destination, what did you see? How did you feel? What were your observations?

3. Jesus says you are like that top. Everyone can see you. There is no hiding. What thoughts go through your mind as you consider being seen as a follower of Jesus?

4. Jesus says you are a light. What does light do? If we are light, what are we called to do in this world? Knowing this, does it convict us in any way to be more like Jesus? If so, how?

5. Jesus calls us to be people who do good things. When you read the Gospel accounts, Jesus is clearly doing good things every day. What margins do you need to create in your life in order to better follow his example? List some things we should be more involved in every day, to look more like Jesus.

6. How can this church better create avenues to "do good things"?

CHAPTER ELEVEN

SENSES:
THESE GIFTS ARE NOT
PURCHASED AT WALMART

*J*am not an engineer in the strictest sense. Oh, I've built my share of childhood forts in the yard and tents in the living room. I've wiggled a few connection cords to get the computer to work again. I've even built an eight-chair-round farmhouse dining room table for my wife. (Gentlemen, let me say, "Happy wife, happy life"!) However, I am consistently amazed at how our postmodern world works.

I get in my Toyota Sequoia, turn the key, and the SUV revs to life, allowing me to get from my house to the airport where I then get on an airplane. I have no real idea how internal combustion works or makes all the pieces of my car work together for my good. But what a phenomenon! I have a personal vehicle that can move me from point A to point B in a flash.

And the airplane! We get all upset because the plane landed late; we had to sit on the plane for thirty minutes awaiting take-off; or because we had to sit in the middle seat between an older gentleman who is already snoring and smells like a burrito, and a dark-haired guy wearing sunglasses who you would swear looked just like the bad guy on last night's episode of *Criminal Minds*.

But have you thought about how incredible it is to fly? What an incredible feat of engineering! Depending on the size of the plane, you are traveling in a relatively straight line, uninhibited by topography, moving from point A to point B at a speed between 575 and 930 mph. I have no idea how that occurs, but am so excited to just think about how quickly all those moving parts on an airplane work together to get me to where I want to go, even faster than my already amazing vehicle!

Even something as simple as a light sensor in a room is great technology. I work at a church where many of the lights in the building simply come on when you enter a room. Of course, there have been issues with all this wonderful technology—for instance, when you're in the bathroom a "little longer" than you had hoped and the lights go off because there has been no movement . . . in every way.

We have a security company that monitors our facility. I'm first on the security phone call tree at church, because I live the closest to our building. Early one morning about 2:00 a.m. I received a phone call letting me know that the police had been dispatched to our facility to answer an alarm. I jumped out of a dead sleep, put on my clothes (thank the Lord I was awake enough to remember to do that), and drove the three miles to the church building.

When I reached the building, I then realized the police had not yet arrived, so I began to walk the perimeter to see if I noticed any broken windows or open doors. Please remember that it's dark outside and the wind is breezy. Oh, and that I am a scaredy-pants who can and will scream like a five-year-old girl if the need arises.

I finally got around to the front door and peered into the darkness of the interior. Only the green exit signs lit up any discernable images in the church common area. There seemed to be no movement inside.

Remember how I was telling you about the automatic lights and how cool they were? Well, about the time I noticed the police rounding the corner to come meet me, I also noticed the light in the women's bathroom coming from under that door in our common area. Are you kidding me? At 2:00 a.m. The church burglar needed a potty break after putting all the left-behind Bibles in her knapsack! (I say "her" because the "burglar" did go in the women's bathroom.)

I showed the police how the light was beaming out from under the bathroom door. Can you believe they asked if I wanted to go in? Of course I said in my most manly voice, "Absolutely . . . *not!*" So they went inside, hands on weapons, flashlights gleaming, and after ten minutes of looking around, came outside and told me they could not find anything. I went in, while they were still there, to discover that nothing was out of place but exactly where it should be. I guess it was a female mouse that set off the cool technology that got me out of bed at 2:00 a.m.

Even in this situation, you've got the technology that alerted the monitoring company who called the police and me to discover that we may have a mouse in the building. The point being, several things are using their given "muscle," working together to accomplish what needs to be done.

In the summer of 2015, Robin and I had the absolute privilege of traveling to Kenya, Africa. Our church supports an orphanage of forty deaf children there called Sam's Place. These are forty of the most loving, smiling, adorable kids with whom you could ever hang out. Each of their pasts contain an incredible story.

These kids are deaf and mute. Their families tossed them out at young ages to fend for themselves. You see, when you have these physical issues in Kenya, especially being deaf and mute, some parents believe there is a demon living inside their child. They don't want anything to do with a child who has a demon, so they put their kids outside the house and say, "good luck." The country of Kenya does not even recognize these children's citizenship. Even so, amazingly, every single morning, these kids go to the flagpole, raise their country's flag, and say the pledge to their country. That's a book in itself!

The Americans who facilitate Sam's Place have gathered all the kids they could help and placed them in this one location. These forty kids are loved and cared for. They are given a bed to sleep in and three meals a day. They are given medicine when it's needed. The girls are taught how to be seamstresses; the guys are taught how to be carpenters. They are taught a trade so that when they leave the orphanage at eighteen years of age, they will be able to earn a living for themselves.

Despite their lack of all their senses, the Sam's Place kids are so full of life and love. They know who Jesus is and proclaim their love for him every day. They have nothing by the world's standards, yet smile ear-to-ear every day because they know they are loved and have been given what money cannot buy.

Robin is an excellent teacher and I, well, I'm good at manual labor. Tell me where to place a sixty-pound rock or how to mix cement and I'll make it happen. When we went over in 2015 to work with Sam's Place, Robin's job was teaching the local teachers how to use current teaching styles to better educate the kids. With limited resources, Robin did an incredible job loving on those local teachers, who daily pour into the Sam's Place kids. She showed those teachers the best ways to get any given lesson to stick in a child's memory.

I got to help lay a foundation to pour a concrete sidewalk. We poured two sidewalks between campus buildings. The sidewalks are always needed during the rainy season, so that kids and teachers alike can move around the compound without getting muddy. I also got to work with others to lay cat-5 cable line, so that computers could be linked for the teachers and students. We dug trenches to lay the pipe and ran wire up in the attic of one of the buildings, which I am certain must have been close in temperature to the oven Shadrach, Meshach, and Abednego endured.

So, what do short-term mission trips, our senses or lack of senses, and how our technology works have in common? I think a biblical perspective is in order. Paul says in his first letter to the Corinthian church:

> A spiritual gift is given to each of us so we can help each other. . . . [A]ll the members [of the body] care for each other. If one part suffers, all the parts suffer with it, and if one part is honored, all the parts are glad. All of you together are Christ's body and each of you is a part of it. Here are some of the parts God has appointed: . . . [messengers . . . proclaimers] . . . teachers . . . those who do miracles . . . healing . . . help others . . . who have the gift of leadership, those who speak in unknown languages (1 Cor. 12:7, 25–28).

Paul uses the analogy of the human body, reminding us that we all cannot do the same things. If we all used the same "muscles" or "senses," we would look pretty silly. We might all be one big eyeball or one bony foot or one large nose. Paul says each of us has been given "Kingdom muscle" that we are called to use for God's glory.

That idea was prevalent in that first-century church. It was a totally different idea that Jesus had in mind when he left the earth. He risked everything, leaving that early church in the hands of men and women to carry on his teaching about how to live together.

The culture in Jesus' day was hedonistic and self-serving. The disciples who followed Jesus looked and lived the total opposite of the culture, living as one and journeying together in life for the benefit of others. Look what Luke reports:

> All the believers were united in heart and mind. They felt that what they owned was not their own, so they shared everything they had, . . . There were no needy people among them, because they would sell property and bring the money to the apostles to give to those in need (Acts 4:32, 34–35).

In other words, all disciples used their "muscle" to help each other on the Christian journey. It gives a different feel to the text that calls us to love the Lord with all our strength and to love our neighbor or fellow journey-people just exactly like we love Jesus. I may not be the best teacher or doctor or miracle-worker or electrician or food-provider or orphanage leader, but together, as the body of Jesus, we make a terrific spiritual body for the cause of Christ.

Have you ever had a desire to do something? You were certain this specific thing was exactly what you wanted to do. No one could dissuade you from moving forward in this one area you knew you were called to be a part. But suddenly, someone with more power, authority, respect, or stubbornness told you that your dream will not happen. They actually needed you to use other talents or abilities for a different job. You were floored. You had your heart set. You were sensitized to do one thing, but now you're told to do something different. It will help the cause. It will bring a fuller message. It will help the group as a whole. It will strengthen the story. You thought you'd play a different part in the story but now you're in a different spot. Reluctantly, you concede and do your part.

That is exactly what happened to one guy (we'll call him Crazy Harry for our story) in Mark 5. It was a pitch-black night, right after a massive storm when the disciples and Jesus landed in a boat in an area called the Gerasenes. They all got out of the boat right where the cemetery meets the water and were immediately confronted by the screams that would make the hair on your neck stand on end. Out of the darkness comes terror—terror in the form of one crazed maniac. Crazy Harry is running at you, screaming, with the strength of the Incredible Hulk. Crazy Harry was already possessed by an evil spirit and lived in the cemetery. The text says, "He was so strong, no one could subdue him" (v. 4). I mean, even when they tried to confine him with chains and shackles, he simply broke them off of his wrist and ankles. Crazy Harry was incredibly strong . . . and insane. That's a combination that could win you a championship football game. But we're not playing football, are we?

We're told that Crazy Harry screamed at the top of his lungs all the time and cut himself with stones so that he would bleed. This is beginning to sound like the scene from a horror movie: screaming, confrontation, dark, cemetery, stormy, blood, chains, demons. When Crazy Harry saw Jesus, he sprinted Jesus' direction with the speed of Usain Bolt to ask a question.

Crazy Harry gets in Jesus' face and demands, "Why are you interfering with me, Jesus, Son of the Most High God?" (v. 7). But Jesus will not be moved. He is the ultimate authority. So calmly and with the complete authority of God, Jesus sends the demon out of the man.

I mean, how long had this man battled his demons? How long had he wanted to be different, but could not find the strength to change? How many nights had he wished for rest-ful sleep but was driven to howling and clanking through the night? How many nights had he longed to find someone who could help him turn his life around? How many tears had he shed hoping to find some salvation?

And just like that, one dark night, Jesus appears. Just like that, the demon is gone. Just like that, Crazy Harry is no longer cray-cray but in his right mind. Just like that, he can finally close his eyes to get some much-needed rest. Just like that, he has a new lease on life—one that is moving him to use his com-mon sense to follow the only man who could or did ever help him. Interesting . . . in every story where Jesus interacts with people or touches people or speaks to people or heals people or raises people, people are changed . . . forever. *Every. Single. Story.*

The text tells us that Jesus and his disciples are leaving the east bank of the Sea of Galilee. The locals are pleading for Jesus to "get out" and stop interfering in their lives (sound familiar?). So Jesus and his disciples are getting back in their boat when who appears but Crazy Harry. The now-not-so-crazy man is get-ting in the boat with Jesus. He wants to be near the Master. He wants to know Jesus more deeply. He wants to follow Jesus to the next destination to tell his story of salvation and redemp-tion. He wants to be part of the entourage. He wants to leave the place with so many horrific memories of who he used to be. But Jesus has a different job for him. Jesus is going to redirect his tenacious personality to another location. Jesus wants him to be a part of the story, but not in the way he was thinking.

Jesus tells Crazy Harry to stay right where he is, and to tell everyone how Jesus totally changed his life . . . literally. So Harry gets cleaned up and starts making his rounds in the Decapolis (an area where there were ten closely knit cities). Harry is now going to be a part of the body of believers who tell everyone how awesomely terrific and powerful Jesus of Nazareth is and how Jesus can change their lives just like he changed . . . *mine*. The story goes on till this day.

So, what is your strength? How do you humbly flex for Christ, figuratively speaking? Are you "working out"? If you had to take an inventory of your gift set, what would you write down? How would you tell your story of Jesus' life-changing message? There is a better way to discover your gift set than a self-inventory. Even so, go to the back of this book right now, and write down what you believe your top three "muscles" are for the Kingdom.

Now, the moment of truth. Ask three people, who you trust and believe know you better than anyone, what they believe your top three gift sets are. (Two of these cannot be family members.) Do that this week. When they've given you their answers, compare them to what you wrote down to see if you're on track. My guess is you may be surprised. Places you never thought "muscle" existed will be the very places others see "muscle" in you.

Our goal would be to develop and use those gift sets or senses and muscle God has given us to love on all the people in our life. Our hope would be to show them the beautiful community of Jesus that the world cannot offer. We are called to imitate Jesus the Christ in every way. We are called, according to Paul, to be the body of Christ here on earth. The way God planned it, working together, we can help each other hear better, see better, walk better, be better representatives for Jesus in a world that desperately needs him.

Are you ready to work out? Right where you're located, are you ready to run the race? Lace up your sneakers. Pull on your favorite college hoodie. Fill up your unbreakable water container. Start stretching. Let's go!

Study Guide for Chapter Eleven: Senses

Read the text:

1 Corinthians 12:7–27:

A spiritual gift is given to each of us so we can help each other. To one person the Spirit gives the ability to give wise advice; to another the same Spirit gives a message of special knowledge. The same Spirit gives great faith to another, and to someone else the one Spirit gives the gift of healing. He gives one person the power to perform miracles, and another the ability to prophesy. He gives someone else the ability to discern whether a message is from the Spirit of God or from another spirit. Still another person is given the ability to speak in unknown languages, while another is given the ability to interpret what is being said. It is the one and only Spirit who distributes all these gifts. He alone decides which gift each person should have.

The human body has many parts, but the many parts make up one whole body. So it is with the body of Christ. Some of us are Jews, some are Gentiles, some are slaves, and some are free. But we have all been baptized into one body by one Spirit, and we all share the same Spirit.

Yes, the body has many different parts, not just one part. If the foot says, "I am not a part of the body because I am not a hand," that does not make it any less a part of the body. And if the ear says, "I am not part of the body because I am not an eye," would that make it any less a part of the body? If the whole body were an eye, how would you hear? Or if your whole body were an ear, how would you smell anything?

But our bodies have many parts, and God has put each part just where he wants it. How strange a body would be if it had only one part! Yes, there are many parts, but only one body. The eye can never say to the hand, "I don't need you." The head can't say to the feet, "I don't need you."

In fact, some parts of the body that seem weakest and least important are actually the most necessary. And the parts we regard as less honorable are those we clothe with the greatest care. So we carefully protect those parts that should not be seen, while the more honorable parts do not require this special care. So God has put the body together such that extra honor and care are given to those parts that have less dignity. This makes for harmony among the members, so that all the members care for each other. If one part suffers, all the parts suffer with it, and if one part is honored, all the parts are glad.

All of you together are Christ's body, and each of you is a part of it.

Open:

Tell a story about a time you hurt a body part—a toe, knee, back, eye. . . . What was it like working around a part of your body that was not functioning correctly? How difficult was it? How did you overcome the deficiency?

Dig in:

1. While acknowledging that Paul's list may not be all-inclusive, list the gifts in this text.

2. Paul says these gifts are given to help each other. Pick a gift from your list and comment on how this gift may be beneficial to the body of believers at your church. Why do you think that is?

3. Paul states that the Spirit alone gives gifts. How would one know what gift they have? How does the body of

believers affirm that gift? If the Spirit has indeed given a gift, do we have the right to not use that gift (see Matthew 25:14–30)?

4. At times, the pastor or church minister is elevated to an honored position. While he/she may be the proclaimer of the weekly message, what would this text say about that idea?

5. Paul reminds the reader that "some are Jews, Gentiles, slave or free." In our current culture within the church, we could carry those dichotomies out to include race, gender, single or married, tattooed or clean canvas . . . the list could go on. The underlying idea is that in Jesus, we are all now one body. No one is more special than another. What are some barriers we need to break personally in order to be more inclusive in our spiritual journey? What are the barriers within our church that need to be corrected and removed, in order to become the church Paul is describing in this text?

6. Paul reminds the reader that if we embrace what Jesus is calling us to live out and we use our gift set for his glory, we'll really live in harmony with each other and the world around us. In our church, what are some perceived areas where we could live more in harmony with one another?

7. How do we, as members of the body of Christ, take care of each other? How do we get outside our circle of friends within the church, to discover other members of the body who need to be cared for?

8. How can this church help all of us better use our gift sets? What can this church do better to allow everyone to use their gifts?

CHAPTER TWELVE

PRESENCE:
MAKE JESUS KNOWN

*J*was so blessed to work specifically with teens and parents for twenty years. From 2000–2012, I had a terrific experience each summer with my great friend, Trent Hawkins. The journey is so much more fun and inviting when you have someone beside you who has all the same life goals you do and who wants to change the world for Jesus Christ. Trent is one of those guys who is fearless, loyal, and an incredibly hard worker. If you ever need real estate in Stillwater, Oklahoma, he is your guy.

Trent and I took teens to a great summer camp called Memphis Workcamp in Memphis, Tennessee. It's an opportunity to get about four hundred teenagers out into the areas of Memphis that need a little happiness, a new look, a hand up. Here's how the camp works: Teens sign up with their home church. The church leader gets online with Memphis Workcamp and sends in paperwork for all of the adults and teens. I almost forgot: Teens pay money to go work for someone else in Memphis. *A. Maz. Ing.* Once the teens get to Memphis, they all gather at a host church where they are assigned a group to work with during the next five days. You may only know one other teen in the group, but the hope is that over the week's worth of work, you make some new friends and build Christian community. And here is what these fairly new Christians who have an entire summer to themselves sign up and pay to go and do.

Teens show up at a house on Tuesday morning, in an older part of Memphis. They pray with and for the homeowner. Typically, the owner is an older person on a fixed income and cannot afford the upkeep needed on the house in which they live. So, these teens get all the ladders out of the trailers and find them a spot somewhere on the outside of the house. They begin scraping the old paint off the house. They do that the entire first day.

I don't know if you have ever scraped a house, but it isn't the most fun thing in the world to do. It's boring, and in Memphis during June it's hot and humid. However, these teens want to serve because that's what Jesus did in his life.

Typically by day two, the groups have the buckets of paint open and have begun the first coat on the house. Days three and four, the teens are still painting, with some of them assigned new and specialized jobs. For instance, one year a group of us noticed a handrail gone on the porch; there was a rock to step down into the yard where wooden steps used to be. There was a lady who was ninety-four years old, living in that house by herself. Needless to say, we got busy. Three of us rebuilt her porch steps and handrail by week's end.

Usually, a handful of teens on Friday replant a flower garden and mulch the area in front of the porch, to add brightness and happiness. I mean, these teens are sweaty, hot, tired, hungry, uncomfortable, but happy! They are happy because they are fulfilling the command of Jesus to "go and do." They are putting feet and hands on their spirituality. They are reminding others that Christians are called to be a presence in the world for good. They have had to put a little muscle in the game. They are making sure their faith is accompanied by doing good things for others. The work they are doing is preparing them for other moments in life when they will need to live out their discipleship by doing for others.

James, the half-brother of Jesus, was a New Testament writer and a leader in the Jerusalem church. He was an in-your-face Christian, who even today challenges us to be different from the world around us. He believed there was more to a faith walk than just words. He believed a profession of Jesus as Lord and Savior moved you to be a *tupos* . . . to make a mark for the cause of Christ. He states:

> [D]o you think you'll get anywhere in this if you learn all the right words but never do anything? Does merely talking about faith indicate that a person really has it? For instance, you come upon an old friend dressed in rags and half-starved and say, "Good morning, friend! Be clothed in Christ! Be filled with the Holy Spirit!" and walk off without providing so much as a coat or a cup of soup—where does that get you? Isn't it obvious that God-talk without God-acts is outrageous nonsense?

> I can already hear one of you agreeing by saying, "Sounds good. You take care of the faith department, I'll handle the works department."

> Not so fast. You can no more show me your works apart from your faith than I can show you my faith

apart from my works. Faith and works, works and faith, fit together hand in glove.

Do I hear you professing to believe in the one and only God, but then observe you complacently sitting back as if you had done something wonderful? That's just great. Demons do that, but what good does it do them? Use your heads! Do you suppose for a minute that you can cut faith and works in two and not end up with a corpse on your hands? (James 2:14–20, MSG).

The challenge is for each of us to balance all the aspects of faith in Jesus to produce a life through the power of the Holy Spirit, to imitate Jesus in every way. James emphasizes that faithfulness to God should include getting off our couches and out of the church pews into the world, to do good Jesus-centered things for a world that desperately needs Jesus and the hope he offers. A relationship with God cannot just be based on believing that Jesus is who he claims to be. Real faith results in actions which imitate God's love for us, who showed us what that love looks like by sending his son Jesus to live among people and have compassion upon them. Looking at how Jesus lived will give each of us the template for how faith in action looks. Faith and good works go hand in hand.

I find the way biblical writers put down their stories is always intriguing. John reminds us that there are so many stories it would be hard to print enough books to contain them. So, how did the New Testament Gospel writers decide what stories to journal as they told the story of Jesus? Why did they group certain stories as we read them?

For example, why does Mark, a Gentile, write about Jesus sending out the disciples, and in the same chapter tell about five thousand men who suddenly show up and need to be fed? Could it be that the disciples still did not really understand what type of Messiah Jesus truly was? Could it be that they thought they were being sent out to recruit followers for Jesus? Could it be that the disciples were telling everyone on their recruiting journey they had discovered the foretold Messiah and that he was going to reestablish Israel? Could the five thousand men (who Jesus eventually fed with two fish and five loaves) really be an assembled army ready to follow Jesus to overthrow the Roman government? If you read the story in Mark 6, you'll discover that after Jesus feeds the huge crowd, he sends the disciples across the Sea of Galilee and then disburses the crowd of men and women who had gathered.

Likewise, I find it interesting in Matthew 25 how Matthew, a Jew, groups three stories. He seems to want to remind the reader that as followers of Jesus, we are called to have a presence in this world, to exert some spiritual muscle. It's more than just following the rules, keeping the Sabbath, not murdering someone, going to church, or not stealing your brother's baseball trading cards. See, Matthew includes three stories in chapter 25. This grouping of stories occurs *right* before the story turns to Jesus' arrest and death. Stories told right before someone dies seem to carry weight, importance. They seem to be a flag waving, bringing attention to the baseline of how someone is feeling.

The first story in Matthew 25 talks about a wedding, and about people who claimed to know the groom (a metaphor for Jesus). They have said all the right things but not used any muscle. Some of the wedding party did not do anything to prepare for the groom to show up. They signed up, said they would show up, promised they would witness the event, but ended up not really doing anything. Their words did not really match up with their actions.

The second story is a mix of those who balance words and action. Three servants were given gifts to use while the master was away. In this story, the master is a metaphor for Jesus. One servant was given five bags of silver, a second was given two bags of silver, and a third was given one bag of silver. The first two invested or put their gifts to work, which doubled their initial investment. They used muscle to add to what the master had already given them. The third was afraid of the master and of losing any of the gift so he simply buried it where it sat and did nothing.

Upon the master's return, each was asked by the master what he did with the gift. The master celebrated with the first two servants because they used the gifts they were given by the master to broaden the scope of the gift. The third, while being honest, revealed he had not used his master's gift at all. So, the master took the one bag of silver and gave it to the servant who had ten bags. The master also sent the third servant out of his presence. See, you get to have a presence if you use your presents.

The third story in Matthew 25 is a reminder that as followers, we are called to sacrifice and serve. You see, that is how Jesus lived his entire life. Read all four Gospel accounts of Jesus' life. You'll see that he never sidestepped his calling to serve and love, to be kind and compassionate, and to be generous and have faith in the Father's plan, which called him to interact with the world around him. Jesus says in this third story, talking to those who said they had the kind of faith in him that called them out of the church pews and off the couch into the world, "I was hungry and you fed me. I was thirsty, and you gave me a drink.

I was a stranger, and you invited me into your home. I was naked, and you gave me clothing. I was sick, and you cared for me. I was in prison, and you visited me" (vv. 35–36).

Those who follow Jesus are quick to ask when they ever saw Jesus in any kind of need. When did they attend to Jesus? When did they help him out? How in the world could they have missed actually realizing they were helping the Son of God? And Jesus says his followers helped him whenever they put their faith to work by helping other people. Jesus literally says you were in his presence attending to him when you decided to put some muscle in your faith. As a follower, when you helped someone who could never pay you back or give you a leg up or give you something in return, that's when you actually were serving Jesus.

Consider those teens who, every June, pay to show up in Memphis and help someone who cannot help him/herself. Consider when they show up to paint a house or build a porch or attach a handrail or trim up a vacant lot or pick up trash on a forgotten street. Those teens are serving Jesus and others. When we use our muscle to bring attention to his name and his plan, we are serving not only others who are created in his image but Jesus as well.

Think about your hometown. Think about the town where you live right now. In the back of this book, list the needs people have in your town. Maybe you have a local homeless shelter, soup kitchen, or homeless church that meets under the overpass on Sundays. It could be that your city has a shelter house for domestically abused women and children, or a pregnancy help center. It's possible you have a once-a-month experience to assist families who have special needs children on a Saturday or a local program for Special Olympics. Maybe you know of a scouting program that assists at-risk kids to become Boy or Girl Scouts.

Go ahead. Write down as many ways you know of that people need help in your community. Go ahead and do that now . . . I'll wait.

You may know of a need that is not yet being met. What a wonderful space God has created for you to unbury that gift and use it for his glory—to be a presence. There are numerous ways you can be a presence for Jesus. You can create the space where faith meets action. Instead of waiting on someone, why couldn't you be the founder of a community-action moment to be the hands and feet of Jesus? It does not have to be a multimillion-dollar nonprofit. Just start. Convince a handful of others just like you that it's time for action. It's time to stop talking about Jesus and go *be* Jesus!

This chaotic, ridiculous, nonjoyous world needs Jesus. And it needs you! With the Holy Spirit inside you and Jesus beside you, nothing can stand in your way to change the world by spreading the hope of Jesus through word and action. Be the positive presence Jesus has called you to be. Don't wait. The world needs to hear and see how Jesus has changed your life for the better. Share that story. Share your life. Share Jesus.

Study Guide for Chapter Twelve: Presence

Read the text:

James 2:14–20:

What good is it, dear brothers and sisters, if you say you have faith but don't show it by your actions? Can that kind of faith save anyone? Suppose you see a brother or sister who has no food or clothing, and you say, "Good-bye and have a good day; stay warm and eat well"—but then you don't give that person any food or clothing. What good does that do?

So you see, faith by itself isn't enough. Unless it produces good deeds, it is dead and useless. Now someone may argue, "Some people have faith; others have good deeds." But I say, "How can you show me your faith if you don't have good deeds? I will show you my faith by my good deeds."

You say you have faith, for you believe that there is one God. Good for you! Even the demons believe this, and they tremble in terror. How foolish! Can't you see that faith without good deeds is useless?

Open:

Have you ever been on a mission trip or helped someone around town through a church outreach? Tell us about the event. How did you feel? What did you accomplish?

Dig in:

1. James is an in-your-face kind of Christian. He believes that faith and doing good go hand in hand. What do you believe about that? Is there a close correlation?

2. Looking at a Christian life from the world's view, why is it important that deeds accompany faith? Does it make a difference?

3. What does Jesus say about faith and works (see Matthew 7:26–27)?

4. In your own words, explain James 2:18.

5. The right motivation is important to understanding the value of work. What are you being asked to do by James, and why (see also 1 John 3:16–18)?

6. Read Romans 3:28. How do Paul's words relate to James' commission? Do they contradict? Why or why not?

7. What margin do you need to build into your life to create better balance between faith and doing good things?

8. How can the church facilitate better ways of reaching out into our community and world to do good things? List your dreams of what a church might be doing that would let Jesus' light shine in the world.

RESTORATION

*J*f you have a dresser in your bedroom, you no doubt have it compartmentalized like I do. I mean, everything has a permanent place and its own drawer. There are folded t-shirts in one drawer, your unmentionables (that's your underwear) in a different drawer. Your socks are located in their own drawer, although both dress socks and casual socks may live in the same drawer. There is even a drawer for memorabilia, keepsakes, and junk you don't know where to put.

Imagine that someone changed the drawers around every day. That would drive you bananas. You came out of the shower on any given morning, went to get a clean pair of undies, and instead you grabbed some dress socks or, heaven forbid, the brochure from a Scottish castle you visited in the late 1980s. Well, that would not do. It would be frustrating. You might even throw something and lose your Christian witness on day three of this ongoing event. Therefore, to avoid all that, you and I have designated drawers for those undies and that doesn't change. We know right where to go and what drawer to pull when we walk out of the shower.

Now let's think about that idea, that concept, but in a much more important sense. In this postmodern culture that you and I live in, did you realize that if we aren't intentional, we live our lives compartmentalized the same exact way? We end up pigeonholing our entire life. We put things in metaphoric drawers so the two things never cross. At just the right moment, we know exactly what drawer to open, depending on the moment.

When we need to attend to a relationship, we know which drawer to open. We have our spouse or girl/boyfriend in that drawer. We have a relationship with our coworkers. We have a relationship with the bank teller we like to use. We have a relationship with our salonist. If we have a "speedy" relationship with our local police officer too often, we may lose our license.

A drawer exists for our entertainment. In that drawer we will find movies, television, social media, magazines, and books. That is where the ballgame we attend on weekends or the Broadway play we love to frequent lives. Anything that occupies our mind for a segment of time could be considered entertainment.

A compartment is there for our finances. How much we are saving or placing in our retirement account lives in this drawer. How much we spend on food or that above-mentioned entertainment is set in that drawer.

There is a drawer for work. The temperament we need to conquer and get things done for the boss lives here. The spreadsheets and computer exist in this drawer. All those miles in the air due to work are right here.

For those of us who follow Jesus, there is a drawer for him as well. On any given Sunday morning, I do not mind the preacher reminding me who he is and what he's done for me. But don't try to put him in another drawer. I have everything right where I want it. Let's not get too crazy and mix things up.

Do you know that in Jesus' day, there was no such thing as compartmentalization for his Jewish audience? Today, we might say, "How is your spiritual walk?" That question would never have been asked among Jews. That's because *everything* was spiritual to a Jewish person. It was just one big dresser drawer. Work was spiritual. Entertainment was spiritual. Relationships were spiritual. Everything was connected to God.

I do believe everything is connected spiritually. One thing doesn't really exist without the other. You may have heard of the book *The Five Love Languages* by Dr. Gary Chapman. He does a great job of reminding us that we all have a language of love, and that when our spouse (or any relationship you have, for that matter) uses your primary love language, you do backflips! When someone does for you what makes you tick, you'll rope the moon for that person (to quote Jimmy Stewart from *It's a Wonderful Life*).

For example, my primary love language is words of affirmation. When my wife encourages me (like she did to write this book), or uses kind words toward me or compliments me, it energizes me. I would do just about anything for her when she praises me, whether I deserve praising or not. (Don't tell her that, because I'm certain I'll have a list of honey-dos waiting for me when I get home.) Affirmation is a great thing for any of us.

But did you know there are four other love languages? There is physical touch, acts of service, quality time, and receiving gifts. What do you think would happen in a relationship if all five were used to build relationship? Can you say explosion? Can you say flourish? If all five languages were used, the relationship would be an incredible work of art. I would never presume everything would be perfect in that relationship, but it would be as close as one could get.

Now, let's change gears. The focus of this book has been Mark 12:29–31, which states:

> Jesus replied, "The *most* important commandment is this: 'Listen [God's children]! The LORD our God is the one and only LORD. . . . [Y]ou must love the LORD your God with all your heart, all your soul, all your mind, and all your strength.' The second is *equally important*: 'Love your neighbor as yourself.' *No other commandment* is greater than these [two]" (emphasis mine).

Some of us may feel that we bring a whole lot of logic to the table when we consider how we relate to God. We study and keep his Word close to us. It's important for us to understand history and culture when studying about Jesus. We feel we have all that covered and feel good about what we have learned.

Some of us feel that emotionally we are connected. Every. Single. Time. We sing "Good, Good Father" by Chris Tomlin, while crying through a box of Kleenex. We raise our hands as we worship on Sunday morning, revealing to God we have an offering for him as we sing his praise. Some of us look at a cross, hang our heads, and wonder how could we have created the moment where Jesus needed to go there and die for us? We are touched and moved in an emotional way.

Some of us were raised not to cry or show emotion in our fellowship. Some of us (especially men) were taught that real men suck it up—just be tough. We may not know a great deal about church history or language. We may not raise our hands on a Sunday but we can cook a hotdog at a youth gathering, or go on a mission trip to Kenya and pour concrete. We have the physical aspect of following down to a tee. That is how we show our love for God.

Some of us may take time to "navel gaze," as we contemplate how God is speaking to us. We may read a thought-provoking book that makes us reconsider a theological direction. Through prayer, we may even feel the Holy Spirit talking to us, moving us, getting us to feel his presence and direction. We may sense the Spirit of God calling us into a certain ministry or location or relationship.

Each one of these paragraphs has been just an example of how each of us loves God through our emotions, spirituality, logical thinking, or even our physical work. But what if we took Jesus' words literally? What if we decided that Jesus meant what he was saying in Mark 12, and that we are called to live out a worshipful life to him in *all four categories*? What if our call from Jesus as his followers was to live the most important thing (loving God and loving people), not only in our primary language but in all four? What would your life look like if you, day by day, lived out the call to exemplify Jesus in *every* component of your life—not just the easy one, not just the one that seems to come naturally?

I believe Jesus calls us to do just that. Jesus says the most important thing (literally, there is no other thing in the universe more important) is to love God in every facet of your life—to love him in every possible way, even the ones that may not come naturally.

You and I are called to love God and express that love through emotion and, in doing so, make a mark for him on this earth with our life song. We are called to experience him spiritually, using all our senses to feel his presence and power around us and through us. We are commissioned to think about him and how he has called us to live in our postmodern culture by understanding the culture, traditions, and language of his day. We are called to be prepared to give an answer for the reason of our hope by committing his Word to memory. You and I are called to live not only in faith but in action as well, loving people who are created in his image, acting compassionately like Jesus when we are with them.

What a beautiful and complete picture we paint when we fully follow Jesus' words, loving God and people with all our heart, soul, mind, and strength. I would love to imagine a world where all of Jesus' followers decided to truly experience God in all four ways. Remember the phrase, "Be the change you want to see in the world"? I believe we have been given the challenge to change not only ourselves through the power of the Holy Spirit, but to change the world in which we live for the glory of God.

So what are you waiting for? You've written a lot of stuff down in the back of this book. Pick two or three items, and see how God starts changing you to love him more fully and in every possible way! Start painting the masterpiece that God has always planned for you to paint.

May God's Spirit be with you as you consider his direction. May you feel the powerful tug of God on you to be a tupos to the world around you. May you glorify God in all that you decide to do with your heart, soul, mind, and strength!

APPENDIX FOR ACTION

Chapter One—*Tupos*: It's Time to Make a Mark

Write down three components of your life right now that are not exactly where you would like them to be. Write down where you would rather your life was in each of those areas of concern:

1. _____
   _____
   _____
   _____
   _____
   _____

2. _____
   _____
   _____
   _____
   _____

3. _____
   _____
   _____
   _____
   _____

Chapter Two—Devotion: How Do You Give Unconditional Love?

Write down your best friend's name, and one detailed reason why you love that person. Then, text or call that person this week to let them know specifically why you appreciate them:

Your Friend's Name: _____

- _____

_____

_____

_____

_____

_____

_____

_____

_____

_____

_____

_____

_____

_____

_____

_____

_____

_____

_____

_____

_____

_____

_____

Chapter Four—Experience: Thank Those Who Have Poured into You and Your Life

Think about the adult(s) who poured into you during your adolescence. How did they affirm you and encourage you? Afterward, text, call, or email them to let them know what they meant to you. No more than three names:

1. _____
   • _____
   _____
   _____
   _____
   _____
   _____

2. _____
   • _____
   _____
   _____
   _____
   _____
   _____

3. _____
   • _____
   _____
   _____
   _____
   _____
   _____

Chapter Seven—Set: Time to Commit to Be in God's Word and Prayer Every Day

Write down your general weekly schedule. When, during your day, will you make time to dig into God's Word to read the story of Jesus?

Sunday: _____

Monday: _____

Tuesday: _____

Wednesday: _____

Thursday: _____

Friday: _____

Saturday: _____

Chapter Ten—Muscle: You Are the Light

If anything was possible, what would you do differently in your life to look more like Jesus? What would you change, if you could better define your faith walk?

_____

_____

_____

_____

_____

_____

_____

_____

_____

_____

_____

_____

_____

_____

_____

_____

_____

_____

_____

_____

_____

_____

Chapter Eleven—Senses: What Gifts and Talents Has God Given You?

Write down what you believe your top three gift sets are from God. This week, ask three people what they believe your gift sets are (only one of them can be a family member).

1. _____

2. _____

3. _____

Who are the three people you will ask?

1. _____

2. _____

3. _____

Chapter Twelve—Presence: How Will You Make Your Presence Known for Jesus the Christ?

Write down the overarching needs of people in your town or city. How many different ways are you aware that people need Jesus—and that you could be his hands and feet?

1. _____

2. _____

3. _____

4. _____

5. _____

6. _____

ENDNOTES

1. *Country Study Guide*, Vol. 1, Strategic Information &
   Developments (Washington, DC: International Business
   Publications, 2013), 46–47.

Connect with Tim at
thetimhall.com